Mary Ann K. Hunt, Psy.D.
2240 Palm Beach Lakes Blvd.
Suite 325
West Palm Beach, FL   33409

W9-BIT-628

YOUR ANXIOUS CHILD

YOUR ANXIOUS CHILD

RAISING A HEALTHY CHILD IN A FRIGHTENING WORLD

Mary Ann Shaw, Ed.D.

A BIRCH LANE PRESS BOOK
Published by Carol Publishing Group

Copyright © 1995 by Mary Ann Shaw
All rights reserved. No part of this book may be reproduced in any form,
except by a newspaper or magazine reviewer who wishes to quote brief
passages in connection with a review.

A Birch Lane Press Book
Published by Carol Publishing Group
Birch Lane Press is a registered trademark of Carol Communications, Inc.
Editorial Offices: 600 Madison Avenue, New York, N.Y. 10022
Sales and Distribution Offices: 120 Enterprise Avenue, Secaucus, N.J.
  07094
In Canada: Canadian Manda Group, One Atlantic Avenue, Suite 105,
  Toronto, Ontario M6K 3E7
Queries regarding rights and permissions should be addressed to Carol
Publishing Group, 600 Madison Avenue, New York, N.Y. 10022

Carol Publishing Group books are available at special discounts for bulk
purchases, sales promotion, fund-raising, or educational purposes. Special
editions can be created to specifications. For details, contact: Special Sales
Department, Carol Publishing Group, 120 Enterprise Avenue, Secaucus, N.J.
07094

Manufactured in the United States of America
10 9 8 7 6 5 4 3 2 1

Library of Congress Cataloging-in-Publication Data

Shaw, Mary Ann.
    Your anxious child : raising a healthy child in a frightening
  world / Mary Ann Shaw.
       p.   cm.
    "A Birch Lane Press book."
    Includes index.
    ISBN 1-55972-318-1 (hardcover)
    1. Anxiety in children.   2. Parenting.   I. Title.
  BF723.A5S43   1995
  649'.154—dc20
                                                    95-4695
                                                       CIP

This book is dedicated with affection to the many kids I've helped with anxiety problems over the years and to many more who may be helped through the shared wisdom on these pages.

CONTENTS

PART III
The Tough Stuff

PREFACE

A GUIDE TO GUILTLESS PARENTING

For twenty years now, I've been helping parents and their kids. I began teaching mentally retarded children in Spring Branch, Texas, in 1959, and later spent ten years as director of psychological services at the Texas Scottish Rite Hospital for Children in Dallas, before devoting my time primarily to private practice. All of my professional experiences over the years have helped me know kids and know parents. My job is to share that knowledge to make your job of parenting easier.

This book is written to help parents with children up to age fourteen, but the earlier parents begin to recognize and address anxiety problems in their children, the better. If you can deal with your child's anxieties at a very young age, you can prevent more serious problems that could require long-term professional help.

A tremendous amount of guilt comes naturally with parenting. "Parent" is a position of extreme responsibility. If everything doesn't go right with a child, parents will often feel that whatever went wrong is their fault. Especially in today's busy world, parents feel inadequate. It's difficult for them to muster the time and resources needed to truly feel that they're there for their children providing both the support and guidance necessary for them to thrive.

It's not my intention for this book to heap more guilt onto the already quite large pile most parents have accumulated. Although it's true that many parents create anxious children by passing along their own anxieties, this book is not an indictment of inappropriate parenting. Instead it's a tool for good parents who want to do everything they can to raise happy, healthy children.

To help let go of guilt, parents need to realize that all babies are not easy to care for. Some infants are cuddly and easy, and others are colicky and difficult. But inappropriate parenting styles can make a less-than-perfect situation worse. It is hard for new parents to understand that they are not at fault if their baby doesn't respond to their particular style of loving or caring. A father having trouble with his twelve-year-old son once told me that he knew when his son was born that they would have problems. As an infant, his child had pushed away from him, and the father never forgot it. He felt rejected then, built that feeling into his overall perception of his child, and carried it with him for years.

Many parents do not have a clue about how to deal with a difficult child. Consider the child who has no problems at school but is a terror at home. With these cases, I often find that the child has become the ruler of the roost. One four-and-a-half-year-old boy would hold his father's reading glasses over his father's cup of coffee, and if told to return the glasses, the child would promptly drop them into the steaming cup. The father's threats and anger only fed the son's behavior. My advice: Don't play the game. Walk over and take the glasses from the child and put them in your pocket.

Another difficult child would not get dressed for preschool in the morning. Every morning was a war of socks and shoes. The parents pleaded and coaxed and finally dressed the child each day. My suggestion: Take the child to school in his pajamas. It will happen only once. As long as the parents dressed the child, he didn't really have to do it by himself.

It's important to understand that parents' behavior does have significant and lasting effects on children. That's why I've written this book—to give parents more knowledge about their role and how their children will respond—or will not respond—to their actions.

When I begin to work with parents, I first talk to them about their expectations for their child. Then I get to know their child and feed back to the parents my impression of the child's personality and character. By listening and learning, I can begin to predict a child's reactions to different situations. I parrot the child's language and responses, which lets parents know that their problems are not novel and that solutions do exist.

Often I find that parental expectations don't fit the child, so my job is to realign expectations. I look at it as changing the family shoe size so feet are more comfortable. With expectations and perceptions in line, children stop behaviors that were problematic and begin to thrive, while parents let go of guilt and relax into parenting.

This book is written to help parents recognize and understand anxiety in their children so that they can do themselves what I do for children in my office. I want to teach parents how not to be anxious and how to focus on their children in a positive way. I want parents to know their children so well that they, too, can predict reactions and responses. Armed with this understanding, parents can act to prevent anxiety in their children or help their children overcome problems with anxiety that already exist.

It's a stressful world we live in, and I want parents to understand that they are not the only ones who are stressed. Kids are stressed, too. But with some effort and a lot of understanding, you can raise a healthy child in an anxious and frightening world.

Throughout the book, various identifying data of all cases discussed have been changed in order to protect the privacy and confidentiality of the patients.

ACKNOWLEDGMENTS

There are innumerable influences on a person's ideas from the first teacher to the last patient, but my experience for ten years as director of psychological services at the Texas Scottish Rite Hospital for Children in Dallas has shaped my career and my thoughts more than any other. When I began my work there, I was ignorant in so many areas. Because of the wide variety of cases I saw, and because I was the only psychologist on staff, I was forced to educate myself well and rapidly. I didn't have the luxury of treating my small patients for months. Sometimes I'd have only a few days or a few weeks to try to help. There could have been no better preparation for today's insurance-driven, results-oriented medical marketplace, where time is always of the essence.

I also want to acknowledge the many students I've worked with in the graduate program of the psychology department of the University of Texas Health Science Center where I am an assistant clinical professor. Their sharing of information and ideas has been a valuable and invigorating influence on my own work.

Also of great importance to this book is the increased research in the field of psychology, which has linked so much of behavior to our genetic makeup. When I received my degrees in the late '60s and early '70s psychologists were deep into the "nature versus nurture" debate. Many leaders in the field of psychology rejected a genetic predisposition to behavioral problems just as they rejected the possibility that many so-called adult psychological disorders existed in children. Now that my field is acknowledging and diagnosing psychological disorders even in toddlers, and is aware that many of these problems are genetic, we can begin preparing parents and helping children much earlier, saving them years of pain and struggle.

I also need to thank the many colleagues who've helped me and my patients over the years, especially pediatricians who increasingly are willing to openly share ideas with psychologists to improve children's lives. In particular, I want to thank Dr. James J. Terfruchte, assistant professor of child and adolescent psychiatry at the University of Texas Southwestern Medical Center, and Cindy Pou, speech pathologist, for their contributions to Chapter 3 of this book.

I thank the many young parents I see who are beginning to use psychology as preventive medicine. It is so smart. But most importantly, I thank the thousands of children I've seen over the years for having faith in me that I could help.

PART I

Recognizing Anxiety
in Your Child

1

Our Anxious Society
WHY IT'S SO HARD TO RAISE CAREFREE CHILDREN

A decade ago, parents didn't have to worry about drinking water causing cancer or about fat or cholesterol or aspartame in a child's diet. Two decades ago, they didn't have to worry about excessive violence on television or in the streets. A kid could ride his bike around the corner to the store for a soft drink and candy without having to watch out for kidnappers or artificial sweeteners. But no more.

Today's kids are afraid of much more than the monster under the bed or in the closet. I see patients who won't go to see a movie with friends or won't go to the mall because they are afraid something might happen to them or to their parents while they're gone. I've seen kids who are afraid they're going to commit suicide, are afraid of being kidnapped, are afraid their parents are going to divorce. The world's problems swirl around us all, and kids are keen observers of the maelstrom.

Anxiety is broadly defined as an emotional uneasiness stemming from the anticipation of danger. It is distinguished from fear in adults because fear is the emotional response to "objective" danger. With children, however, anxiety and fear are basically the same. To a child, "objective" danger or real danger

3

and irrational or perceived danger are often the same. In other words, with a child, fear is fear.

Fear, however, is certainly not all bad. It is a God-given emotion that serves as an important survival tool. Fear is a natural feeling, one that lets us know we need to take care of and protect ourselves. Psychologists call it the fright/flight response because our natural reaction to fear is to turn away from it. Fear has even been known to trigger superhuman responses, such as the mother who suddenly finds the strength to lift a car off of her child.

As adults, we unknowingly teach fear to children from the time they are infants. The first games we play are of the "peek-a-boo" and "I'm going to get you" variety. Think about the lyrics of Rock-a-bye Baby: "... when the wind blows the cradle will fall." That's not exactly a comforting notion. As children mature, we read them fairy tales about wolves eating Red Riding Hood, wolves blowing down pigs' houses, and butchers' wives cutting off the tails of blind mice.

Before we became such a fearful society, these stories might have seemed tame. But with real fears all around us, we perhaps should reconsider the way we entertain and soothe our children to sleep.

Parents can use bedtime to begin teaching relaxation techniques to their children. Hum softly to them or rub their backs while you coax them to breath slowly and deeply. If the dark makes them tense, turn on as many lights as they need. Make a nightly prayer one of protection rather than using old standbys such as "Now I lay me down to sleep" that have scary lines such as "If I should die before I wake..." Make a game out of identifying night noises by taking turns naming the sounds. "I hear a bird," "I hear a limb scratching the roof," "I hear a dog barking."

Children are no different than adults when they're getting ready to go to sleep. When all of the stimuli of the day begins to fade and we turn out the lights, we are all left to our own vulnerabilities.

THE BAD NEWS

Now we know so much about society's dangers—from the moment they occur. We live in an information society, and much of the information disseminated so quickly via Fedex, fax, E-mail and television is bad. The world's disasters are beamed into our living rooms instantaneously. War, earthquake, famine, terrorism—we see it all as it happens. Every network has one or even two newsmagazines searching for stories on failed product safety, the newest environmental hazard, or the disease of the week. Local news stations have sophisticated helicopters to "get there first" to the scene of disaster and bring the news back to us minute by minute.

Understandably, parents are worried, and, unfortunately, they pass their own anxieties on to their children. Often these anxieties are hidden behind angry behavior. When parents have strong fears, they are often too restrictive of their children's freedom. As a result, they get a lot of back talk. Their children are angry because their parents haven't taught them how to be independent and have interfered with their developmental progress.

An abundance of bad news is just part of the reason why anxiety in children has become the "Disease of the '90s." Estimates of the prevalence of anxiety in children vary greatly, with some studies suggesting 1 to 2 percent of children suffer from anxiety and others indicating as much as 16 percent of children are anxious.

The idea that many of us are "normally" anxious because of the world around us was first asserted by Dr. Rollo May in the 1950s. May was one of the first psychologists to believe that we suffer from anxiety because there is a lot to be anxious about, and that we are not "crazy" if we have anxious feelings.

Before the 1950s, all anxiety was thought to be neurotic, and May's work helped to clarify the difference between neurotic and normal anxiety. During the '50s, fears ran high due to a perceived nuclear threat, and many psychologically healthy people suffered from generalized anxiety as a feature of normal life. Although nuclear threat has subsided in recent years, the rise of violent crime has put many urban dwellers back in a war-zone frame of mind where heightened anxious feelings are certainly the norm.

Today, researchers theorize that anxiety, a constant troubled state of mind that is to some degree debilitating, is caused either by a single serious traumatic event in one's life or by a series of smaller traumas or stresses. Certainly the reality of today's world—especially in urban areas—feeds both of these theories. Whether anxiety is caused by a single event, a series of stresses, or both, our world offers plenty of cause for anxiety.

Research also indicates that anxiety in children is an inherited trait. A 1990 study of twenty-one children and adolescents suffering from obsessive-compulsive disorder concluded that 15 of the children studied had a parent with either obsessive-compulsive disorder or obsessive-compulsive symptoms.[1]

Anxiety is now being recognized as a more common and more serious problem in children than was previously thought. Studies have found that as much as 20 percent of school-aged children exhibit internalizing problems such as anxiety. The increasing number of children I see with anxiety problems in my private practice alone makes me suspect that the real numbers are higher than studies indicate and are growing.[2]

Anxiety in children has been underrecognized and undertreated in the medical community in part because parents don't immediately seek help for "internalizing" problems such as anxiety. Parents are far more likely to seek treatment or help for a child who acts out or who exhibits aggressive behavior than for a child who withdraws.

Part of the blame for underrecognizing and undertreating anxiety in children also falls upon the medical community. Until fairly recently, within the past five to ten years at least, the medical community has not fully accepted that "anxiety" is a diagnosable state for children. In 1987, for the first time, the American Psychiatric Association Diagnostic and Statistical

Manual of Mental Disorders allowed for the potential diagnosis of all adult classifications of anxiety disorder to apply to children. Since that time, many studies have agreed that all anxiety disorders found in adults do occur in children. Similarly, these studies have shown that children who suffer from anxiety are likely to have related or more severe anxiety problems as adults.

Anxiety is crippling for children. It is far more serious for them than for adults because adults can understand anxiety and therefore find ways to deal with it, while children often cannot comprehend why they are feeling anxious. For a child, "I am afraid" is the most limiting of feelings and can often be completely debilitating. The effects of anxiety are multifaceted: studies have shown that anxiety not only hurts academic achievement but also can stifle social development.

Kids who are naturally shy or reticent have a problem developing socially because their anxiety gets in the way. They may go up to a group of kids who are talking, but rather than jumping right in, they begin to rehearse what they are going to say. While they are rehearsing, the conversation moves forward, so what they were going to say no longer fits. Then they begin to feel anxious that too much time has passed and they haven't said anything. They imagine that everyone else is thinking this also and they become too paralyzed to speak.

Children who suffer from anxiety may only try a new activity such as soccer or gymnastics once after much prodding by parents. Anxiety to perform well without learning the skills creates such pressure. These children will quit the team in order to reduce the anxiety. They'll withdraw socially and then they won't have the experiences needed to help them mature. Similarly, in school, if an anxious child fails a test miserably, even if the rest of the class did, too, it is likely to cause even a very bright child to begin to do poorly on future tests.

Anxiety has a paralyzing effect on kids. It is as if they stop their development at the onset of severe anxiety. I see this time and time again in families where the parents either are divorcing or should be divorcing. Children in these families stop their emotional development at the onset of the extreme anxiety, staying "babies." They stop growing and maturing at the point where they feel the safest, as if there is so much change in their family that any change within themselves is just too frightening. When the family crisis passes or is resolved, the child begins to mature again.

If anxiety in children goes untreated, it can lead to more serious problems. With adolescents, I continue to see anxiety lead to the use of drugs and alcohol as teens attempt to escape from the anxiety they have lived with since a very early age. And anxiety in children can lead to severe internalizing problems in adulthood such as panic disorder and agoraphobia. Studies continue to indicate that adults with these problems suffered from anxiety as children.

THE INFORMATION OVERLOAD

The proliferation of anxiety in children can be attributed not only to society's problems, which are so evident in our evening news, but also to the vast amount of information about development and mental and physical health that is thrown at parents every day. Parents' desires and concerns for optimum child development have reached a nearly frenzied level in American society. Countless books and television shows espouse endless pos-sibilities when it comes to furthering child development. Parents can no longer feel comfortable with simple facts of yesteryear such as "carrots are good for eyesight." Now parents are asked to consider a plethora of nutritional choices while their child is still in the womb. Some experts recommend playing music and reading to a child long before it is born and starting flash cards even before a child can crawl or walk, much less speak. The by-product of this extreme interest, what some call "hot housing" kids, is not a generation of superhuman children but a generation of anxious children.

Parents are vulnerable to these societal pressures because

they feel inadequate anyway. If an expert on television tells them that allergies lead to hyperactivity, then they immediately take their child to an allergist. Today's world communicates to parents that they can't make mistakes or let their children have accidents. We are inundated with advice, products, and precautionary measures to prevent injury and harm. Advertisements and news programs alike seem to tell us: "Your child wouldn't have had a concussion if she had the wonderful bicycle helmet just developed."

Of course a vast amount of good has come out of our advancements in safety and our increasing knowledge of child development. However, this advanced state has a limiting by-product for our children that can lead to anxiety—it has safety-strapped their freedom.

THE LOSS OF FREEDOM

Children of the '50, '60s and '70s had a tremendous amount of freedom. But since safety is such a concern in cities and towns across this country, more and more rules and limitations have been heaped upon children. Children are carefully instructed not to talk to strangers. They are taught at ever-younger ages about "bad touching" and "good touching." In many neighborhoods, parents may be uncomfortable letting a child ride his bike around the block. All for good reason. Today a child's activities are organized, planned, and plotted on an hourly calendar. Gone is the time when children finished their homework and then just went outside to play.

The result of this atmosphere of fear and structure is that parents say "no" to their children with increasing frequency. The explanation that follows is often a threatening one—"No, it's not safe."

THE ECONOMIC CRUNCH

Anxiety in children is also economically induced. With unemployment, corporate downsizing, and general economic uncertainty, an increasing number of families suffer due to a lack of job security. In spite of an expanding economy, we are told by various government agencies that the rich are getting richer, and the poor are getting poorer, while the middle class is stretched even thinner. It's easy to forget that children experience the loss of comfort and status and the turmoil of change during times of financial difficulty just as parents do.

The simple but sad result of today's environment is that more children are anxious and frightened and fewer are carefree and happy. The good news is that parents can help to reduce anxiety in children through good communication and good parenting. Often kids' anxiety is heightened when parents try to brush past conversations about world problems, neighborhood crime, or their own changing financial status. It is important to talk about opinions and concerns rather than let even small children overhear parts of anxious phone conversations between adults.

LOGICAL PARENTING

When parents allow their children to see the whole picture, and talk about it openly and honestly, it does not cause alarm, but rather reduces anxiety. The best way to deal with the hard reality of our day is to be better parents—not after witnessing problems in children but from the beginning of their lives.

I try to teach parents common-sense, no-nonsense parenting skills that they can take with them from my office to their home. This logical way of parenting enables parents to ease their own anxieties and guilty feelings. Following are some typical childhood problems and my practical solutions to help good parents be better parents.

Problem: My child has trouble at school following the rules. She can't handle it on the playground and bites and kicks.

This is the voice of a worried parent whose four-year-old girl was on the verge of being expelled from preschool. It is very difficult for parents to control their children when they are two or more miles away at school. But one of the things they can do is encourage the teacher to remove their child from the difficult situation before the behavior happens. If their child can't handle it on the playground, the teacher can have them sit out first for five minutes of observation time. (This technique also works at home if a child is having trouble playing with the neighborhood kids or with siblings.)

During the observation time, the teacher or parent could say to the child, "Just look around. Do you see someone else kicking or biting? I want you to watch and see that you are the only one who does this." At the end of the five minutes, ask the child if she can handle the situation. If she says she can, then let her experience it again. If she can't, start over with removal. I also check procedures at home when this behavior is exhibited. I encourage parents to eliminate their own aggressive behavior at home—no roughhousing or spanking.

Always treat children as though they have intelligence. Ask them if they think they can play with the other children without kicking and biting. Let them decide when they are ready so that they will learn to control their own impulses.

Problem: My child doesn't listen to me.

This is a complaint I hear from many parents of six-year-olds. First graders want to try everything on their own, and if you persist in teaching them, they will tune out your lessons.

When children are younger than six, most parents recognize they have short attention spans, so parents give short lessons. As their children get older, parents become more verbal and extend the lessons into chapters and books. Kids tune out the droning "teacher" and sit there, eyes glazed. while a parent expounds. The parent is flat wasting time.

Lessons should be short and to the point. Don't get repetitive or be overly judgmental. Listen to yourself. The classic verbiage of parents whose children tune them out is, "Yes, but...": "Yes, it's great you've dressed yourself, but your shirt doesn't match your shorts." "You didn't do it right" is what your child hears. Parents need to let kids make mistakes and try things their way as long as it doesn't hurt them. To lead children to alternative behaviors without being judgmental, practice language that echoes your child: "Boy, that really must have hurt when the kids wouldn't play with you after you argued with Tommy. I wonder what would have happened if you'd just stopped to think. I bet you never would have said those things to Tommy in the first place. Maybe if you talk to him first thing in the morning..." First describe what the child is experiencing and then talk about alternative behavior using exploratory language. "I wonder" is a good way to start.

Problem: I don't know what's going on in my kid's head.

This is a common parental complaint, and it is a direct result of parents who don't listen to their kids. If you always have an answer for everything, your child is not going to tell you anything. Why? Because you are ready to tell them they're wrong and correct them. As a result, you've convinced your child that you couldn't possibly understand their position. Your child will logically come back with "You don't know my teacher," or "Kids are different now than when you were young."

By being supportive instead of all-knowing, your children will begin to open up to you. Language like "What if..." and "I don't know, what do you think?" invites children to find their own answers.

Also, another question a parent asks everyday is "How was school today?" Ninety-nine percent will answer "Good." Out of frustration, a parent will follow with another useless question, "What did you do today?" This will be answered with "Nothing." The reason for this response is that most school days are standard; the same subjects, the same teachers. Basically, the child experiences nothing new. Talking about your day is a better way to fill the silence. It gives your child time to unwind and then open up to you.

Problem: *I don't know when my child is telling the truth.*

The best way to know when your child is being truthful is to double check him. Children often lie about whether or not they have finished their homework. Start by letting them know that you are going to check the validity of what they tell you. Let your child know that since there has been a problem with this, from time to time you are going to call their teacher and make sure you are being told the truth.

The comfort zone of parenting is trust, and when trust is jeopardized you have to get it back. Telling your child you are going to check up on what she says periodically is the first step toward developing trust. Again, treat your child as though she has intelligence. Tell her that you want and expect her to be honest with you. When you know she is being honest, you'll trust her again. Since children often step off the curb, shorten your trial trusting time to two weeks, then award trust again. Sometimes lying is how a child who tests limits avoids being disciplined. Good liars don't get caught right away.

Problem: *How do I discipline my child and get results?*

Most parents' problems with discipline stem from their dreaming up punishment the moment of the "crime." All crimes seem greater in times of anger, so this method of punishment is not only inconsistent but is usually too harsh. In the child's eyes, the parent is being vindictive. The child is right and will naturally act resentful.

Discipline works best when it is planned ahead of time. The child then knows up front the consequences of certain behaviors and after experiencing the punishment is less likely to repeat the offense. Consider the following "Crime and Punishment" chart as an example. It's good practice to post this type of chart where everyone can see it, for instance, on the refrigerator door.

Crime	Punishment
Talking back or foul language	No TV for a day

Hitting friends or siblings	Can't play together for 20 minutes
Not doing what we ask	Sit in a boring place for 2 to 10 minutes
Leaving the yard without asking	Can't play outside for one day

This type of "Crime and Punishment" chart works well until about age ten. Then the punishment expands to "privileges" and grounding of various forms. ("You didn't do what we asked you to do, so you can't go to the mall today." "You talked back to me, so you can't have the keys to the car tonight.")

Problem: My child wants to negotiate every step of the way.

We can blame this one on a parenting guru of a decade ago who told us all that we were too dictatorial with our children and that we were not teaching children to use their own innate intelligence if we didn't let them negotiate. Bad mistake. What negotiation does is rob you of your power as a parent. Your life will soon turn into a debate class, and you can count on your child having the energy to filibuster you right to your knees.

To children, negotiating is a game. They will play you like a highly paid attorney in a deposition and by getting you to explain each of your points, you'll end up telling them too much. The more words you use, the more ammunition you give them.

Simply do not negotiate. You make the rules in your household. You can stick by them. Don't be suckered into answering pleas of "why?" Rely on the old adage, "Because I said so." Then later in the day, when the moment is long gone, explain the reason for your answer so that your child understands what is behind the rule.

Problem: My child's room is a mess.

Up front, don't have unreasonable expectations for your children. Organization is a neurological skill and some people are more refined in the area of organization than others. If your kid doesn't have that knack, if his skill of organization is not well-defined, then don't expect him to do something he isn't good at doing.

That doesn't mean you can't deal with the messiness. Try a Saturday Bag. Ask your child to pick up his room and his stuff elsewhere in the house. Then go around the house and into his room and everything not picked up goes into the Saturday Bag. On Saturday, rotate out items your child wants to play with. It won't be long before your child catches on.

Problem: My child can't make a decision on what to play with and pulls out all of her toys at once.

In many cases, children do this not because they are naturally messy, but because they can't enjoy one toy or game without getting distracted by another. The answer is simple: limit your child's choices and she will play better. Put up a lot of toys and let your child switch out used for not-used toys every several weeks.

Problem: My child won't take no for an answer.

With many children, "No" is a challenge. There are a couple of simple strategies for eliminating this point of argument. Calmly tell your child, "You will do what I tell you to do." Wait for the time of challenge to subside. Be silent. Miraculously, it works! Don't bribe. Don't give them choices, or you'll be stuck negotiating every step you take.

Another option is to say yes. Try (where it applies), "Yes, you can have dessert after you finish your dinner." "Yes, you can go out and play after you finish your homework." "Yes, you can watch cartoons after you've taken your shower and gotten ready for school."

Problem: My child throws a fit in the grocery store.

Leave your basket immediately. Take your child by the hand

and silently lead him to the car. Get in and drive home. Institute "time out" without a major discussion. If you already have Crime and Punishment rules, this falls under doing what is asked of him.

Institute the punishment from your chart. Leave your child at home with a sitter, your spouse, or a neighbor for the next several grocery trips. Then ask him if he thinks he can handle going to the grocery and behaving well. If he says yes, reward him with the trip, not a treat at the store. If you've fallen into that habit of buying a treat or more than one on each grocery trip, this is a good opportunity to break that habit.

My child throws a fit in restaurants.

Don't take your child out to restaurants until manners have been taught at home. Playing at a restaurant is only appropriate at McDonald's. Make sure your child understands the rules and learns the behavior correctly before placing her in a situation she may not be able to handle. If the child reacts badly, remove her from the situation just as in the grocery store. Try playing "restaurant" at home to learn the behavior. Most small children will remember how to play the game. Teach your child how to talk to the waitress and waiter and how to say please and thank you. She should do this for you, too.

Problem: My child pretends he is sick to get out of going to school.

Once you are certain that he is not ill, treat the child as though he is sick. Put him in his room with the lights out and no TV. Explain that the doctor says TV will hurt his eyes. The behavior will stop immediately because staying home as a ploy will no longer be fun.

Problem: My child is aggressive and strikes out when she is angry.

Often, you teach this behavior to your child. If you use

spanking too often, you teach aggression. I do believe in spanking, but used correctly, you only have to implement it once or twice a year. If your child screams at you, listen to yourself. Often our children's behavior mirrors our own. We have to change before we can expect them to follow.

2

Anxiety and Temperament
WHEN TO PUSH AND
WHEN *NOT* TO PUSH

Temperament is a person's distinct nature or character that has great influence on personality and behavior. Every child is born with a unique temperament—aggressive or shy, outgoing or introverted, active or sedate, and everything in between. Many studies over the last few decades have prompted the psychological community to believe that temperament is both a stable trait, one that lasts throughout a lifetime, and an inherited trait that is determined by each child's gene pool.[1]

From infancy, it is important for parents to read their child's temperament and to form expectations based on their child's unique makeup. When parents try to change a child's temperament, they can exacerbate problems with anxiety.

If parents can become aware of a child's temperament in the youngest stages of development, even from infancy, many problems can be avoided. Most parents think their infant cries because he is tired or hungry, never considering that the child could be crying because of a low frustration tolerance. Try to avoid labels such as "good baby" and "fussy baby." Rather, think of babies as having a high or low level of tolerance. The babies who have a low level of tolerance may have a naturally anxious temperament.

READING YOUR CHILD'S TEMPERAMENT

You can begin to learn about your child's temperament from the moment he or she comes into this world. Babies who cry a lot may not be able to tolerate discomfort. A baby's ability or inability to wait to be fed or have a diaper changed is an indication of how she will deal with frustrations throughout life. Some infants can't stand loud noises. That does not mean that these babies were traumatized at some point in their young lives by being exposed to loud noises, but that they are having reactions that are entirely natural for them. Other babies can sleep through a riot and are not disturbed in the least by the noise.

Some infants show a strong preference for the primary caretaker. They don't like change. As these infants grow up, they may continue to have trouble with change and will not try anything new, whether it's a different fruit or vegetable or a new situation. Still other parents have infants who are happy with whomever is holding them, who are just as comfortable in a car seat in the grocery store as they are in their own bed in their own room. As these children grow up, they are likely to continue this type of easygoing, adaptable behavior.

All of these behaviors are clues to basic temperament. It is important for parents to remember that there is nothing *wrong* with a naturally anxious temperament in a child. However, when parents try to take anxious children and make them something they are not, such as encouraging a timid child to act aggressive or exposing a shy child to a new situation too quickly, it can often make children and parents alike more anxious.

I once treated a twelve-year-old boy who was brought to me because he cried all of the time. He would try to sit in his mother's lap and would sob regularly. After talking with the boy, I learned that his father was trying to teach him to box, be aggressive, and never cry. His dad had grown up in a time and place where street fighting was the norm, and so, whenever this boy would have a problem at school, the father wanted him to solve it by punching out the opponent. However, this was a boy with a shy and sensitive temperament. His father's boxing lessons and constant goading made the boy terribly anxious and prompted the crying episodes.

Through our therapy for the whole family, I convinced the father to back off the physical discipline and the boy's anxiety eased. This wasn't an easy solution. It was tough to persuade the father—who had an aggressive temperament—that although being physical may have worked as a tool for problem solving for him, it was the wrong tack for his shy boy.

One of the most useful psychological studies of tempera-ment, which indicated that temperament is stable over time and significant to psychological development, is the New York Longitudinal Study undertaken by Stella Chess, M.D., and Alexander Thomas, M.D.[2] The study began in 1956 and followed 133 subjects from two to three months of age through adulthood. The study identified nine categories of temperament:

- *Activity Level*, the amount of physical activity compared to sedentary time
- *Rhythmicity*, the regularity or irregularity of biological functions including sleep, feeding, and digestion
- *Approach or Withdrawal*, the character of responses to initial introduction to a new person or thing
- *Adaptability*, how the child responds to manipulation of behavior responses
- *Threshold of Responsiveness*, reactions to sensory influ-ences such as noise level, heat, cold, etc.
- *Intensity of Reaction*, the energy level of responses such as crying or laughter
- *Quality of Mood*, bright or dark tendencies of mood
- *Distractibility*, how hard it is to distract a child from a task
- *Attention Span and Persistence*, how long a child can stick with an activity or how long it takes a child to return to an activity after being distracted from it

Using these measures, the researchers identified three categories of children, the easy child, the difficult child, and the slow-to-warm-up child. The easy children were regular in their biological functions, responded well to new situations, were highly adaptable to change, had mild or moderately intense expressions, and experienced mostly positive moods. They were easy to manage, had regular sleep and feeding patterns, were easy to toilet train, and adapted well to school. About forty percent of the study group fell into this category.

The difficult children were opposite in many of these measures. They had irregular functions, were difficult to toilet train, withdrew from new situations, adapted slowly to change, and were loud and emotional. They were difficult to take care of, and, the researchers noted, mothers often blamed themselves for these problems. About ten percent of the study subjects fell into this category.

The slow-to-warm-up children also withdrew from new situations, were slow to change, and had many negative moods. These children were sometimes irregular in their bodily functions and sometimes not. They expressed moods in a range from mild to intense. They were not as difficult to manage as the difficult children. The researchers described them as "shy" but able to adapt to newness. About fifteen percent of the study group fell into this category.

About thirty-five percent of the children studied showed a mixture of these traits and did not fall clearly into any of the three categories. Taking this study as a fairly representative sample of children, you can easily see that many parents will have to deal with anxious children. The subjects in this study did serve to confirm that temperament is stable over time, yet the study also indicated that environment can and does influence temperament. What I hope to do for parents is show how the right environment and parental influences can be helpful to development and ease anxiety in children, especially the difficult children.

Parents of children with anxious temperaments need to stop and look at themselves, examine their own personalities, that of their parents and their own siblings, and try to determine if their child's behavior is related to general inherited temperament. When you can identify similar behaviors in your child and yourself, your spouse, or someone within your immediate families, these behaviors can often be indicative of genetic temperament.

DEFINING TEMPERAMENT WITH AN ADOPTED CHILD

With adopted children, the personality of the biological parent is an indicator of the child's temperament. However, the Colorado Adoption Project, which compared twelve-month-old babies to both their biological and adoptive parents on various aspects of temperament, found only a "moderate" correlation between a child's temperament and the personality of the biological parent. I advise adoptive parents, however, to gather as much information as possible on the biological parents of their child to help them with child rearing.

Adoptions have changed for the better over the last few decades. As we learned more about the relationship between heredity and good health care, most adoption agencies began to provide a complete medical history of the biological parents of an adopted child. It is very important, however, also to try to obtain a psychological history of both biological parents, including a description of the temperament of both parents, to give adopted parents more information that will be useful as they raise their child.

Parents of adopted children need to be keen observers of their children as infants, noting frustrations and sensory responses that will help them better understand their children as they grow up. The following guidelines can help all parents read the temperaments of their children.

DISTINGUISHING BETWEEN
TEMPERAMENT AND ANXIETY

Ask yourself the following questions to help distinguish between an anxious temperament and an anxiety problem.

1. How often and how easily does your infant/child become frustrated throughout a normal day?
2. Is your infant/child flexible to change of environment or feeding times?
3. Does your infant/child have tolerance for various noises and noise levels?
4. How quickly must your infant/child have needs met?
5. Does your toddler express extreme frustration in not being able to communicate?
6. What degree of frustration does your toddler express with various developmental stumbling blocks such as learning balance or coordination?
7. How does your child respond to new people and situations? Does he/she withdraw from or embrace newness?

Children who become frustrated easily and often, who respond poorly to change of environment or feeding time, who cannot tolerate noise, must have their needs met immediately, express extreme frustration with inability to talk or walk while learning, and who withdraw from new situations are in all likelihood naturally anxious children.

If your infant or child does not exhibit these behavior patterns on a regular basis and is not naturally anxious, then suddenly begins to withdraw, become shy, or express anger, which is often a cover-up for a feeling of anxiety, you can begin to look at your child's environment and experiences to determine what might be the cause of these anxious feelings.

Children who have an anxious temperament cannot tolerate surprises and frustrations. I often use Nintendo as a diagnostic tool. It is a great way to test frustration tolerance. Kids who have absolutely no tolerance will avoid it altogether by refusing to play. The original Mario Brothers games have just enough enemies and traps to test children with an anxious temperament. The games demand that they plan ahead and that they not be easily startled if they want to win. The game will bring out anxious behaviors and I can begin to see how these children probably behave in a classroom either with peer frustration or performance frustration. When they "die" or lose the game the first time, their comments tend to be "I did okay" or "I almost made it." Then as their frustration heightens, they graduate to "That's a stupid game" or "That character is dumb." Their voices start getting louder and their comments more severe: "I hate that character" or "That character is so stupid." Finally they begin using whatever bad language is popular at school—"poo-poo head" or "penis breath"—and their voice escalates until they have an explosive reaction such as throwing the controller to the floor or crying.

Children with anxious temperaments are especially prone to what psychologists call "generalized anxiety disorder." It is important to understand that there are many degrees of anxiety and that some anxiety is good. Good anxiety motivates you to do better and to be productive. But when anxiety starts working against your child, that's when it becomes a disorder. What that means is that the anxiety is interfering with your child's success in life, interrupting progress and achievement and making him uncomfortable. The simplest way to describe generalized anxiety disorder in children is that they are uncomfortable in many kinds of situations.

If you cannot determine whether your child's anxious behavior is inherent or psychological, if it is good anxiety or bad anxiety, consider talking to a professional. Not only will this help keep you from feeling guilty, it may save you from complicating the problem by having mismatched expectations for a naturally shy or anxious child.

CHOOSING THE RIGHT ENVIRONMENT
FOR AN ANXIOUS CHILD

If you try to change a shy child, you can expect to create more anxiety not only for your child but for yourself. You may never be able to change a shy child, but you can learn how to provide the right environment to help this child thrive on his own terms.

Anxious kids have a need to predict situations. They want to know what is going to happen before it happens, and parents can help them do this. Anxiety is a fear, pure and simple. Fear of what? With naturally anxious kids it's often the fear of "I don't know." Anxious kids may be bossy with their friends because defining the play—who is going to play and how they are going to play—helps them feel in control. Some kids want to eat the same thing every day or wear the same pair of jeans every day because the sameness makes them feel more comfortable and in control.

A child who does not want to play soccer, does not like the circus because of the noise, or is a picky eater because of a fear of the unknown doesn't have to sit alone at home every day. After you understand your child's temperament, you can learn to work with the temperament rather than against it to help expose him to new experiences.

MAKING NEW EXPERIENCES FAMILIAR

If you have a child who is afraid of going to school, you can soften the blow of the first day by taking her to school before school starts to walk the halls or meet the teacher. Take your child to the lunch room and to the library. Let your child play on the school playground during the summer and on weekends so that the school becomes familiar territory. By taking children to these places when they don't have to stay there, you can ease their first-day anxiety.

For children who are afraid of playing soccer or taking

gymnastic classes, test the waters with private instruction. If you can foster a feeling of confidence, your child may decide that participating sounds like fun.

Naturally shy or anxious kids don't want to hear "what they are missing." It is natural for parents to want their children to enjoy activities that they found enjoyable as children, but it is important for parents to realize that their child may have different styles of play, different interests, and a different temperament than they have.

After your child tries a new activity, choose a private time to talk about it. Go over what your child's apprehensions were and emphasize that the experience went well. Let your child know that you understand it was hard to relax into the experience, but in the end, nothing bad happened, everything was okay.

LETTING THE SHY CHILD SAY "WHEN"

Guiding a child into successful play does not mean pushing them into a group of children when they are sitting on the sidelines. Shyness and anxiety are painful for children. No child enjoys hugging the wall rather than participating. Pushing shy children into joining the other kids will only make them feel worse. Asking a child, "Why don't you go talk to the other children?" sends two negative messages: first, that they are inadequate and their parents are displeased with them, and second, that they are dumb or don't know how to behave.

The key to successfully encouraging a shy child is to let him take the initiative when he is ready and to help him get ready. It's important for parents to avoid repetitive preaching and encouraging and to simply speak to their children like the intelligent human beings they are.

To determine when shyness or anxious behavior is damaging self-esteem or development, parents must put away their own wishes for what they want their child to be and focus on their child's needs. If a child is comfortable watching from the sidelines, don't push. But when you notice signs of sadness and withdrawal, the drooping head and dragging feet, that is your clue that shyness has become a real problem that needs to be dealt with.

Consider this scenario: Suzie and her mother are shopping at the mall and Suzie doesn't speak to one of her mother's best friends. Instead of chastising Suzie for embarrassing her, or coaxing, "Say hello to Mrs. Johnson, Suzie," Suzie's mom should wait for a quiet time to say something like, "Today when we saw Mrs. Johnson and you didn't speak to her, I bet that was hard for you." This statement, rather than increasing Suzie's pain, should encourage her to talk about the situation and can open up a dialogue between mother and daughter about ways Suzie could have dealt with her shyness. Suzie's mom could make suggestions about how Suzie might be more comfortable speaking to an adult the next time. I think parents are most successful when they make these suggestions in the form of a question, such as, "What if you start with saying good-bye when I say good-bye" or "What if you start out by just smiling when I say hello?" After enough talking—as opposed to being told what to do—Suzie should begin to come up with ideas of her own, feel more comfortable with herself and less panicky about the next time she's faced with a similar situation.

MAKING PLAYTIME CHILD'S PLAY

Children with an anxious temperament often have trouble playing with other children. Again, they feel the need to be in control of a situation. They like sameness, not change. They want predictable outcomes. So going to another child's house to play is terrifying. Similarly, when a child comes over to the anxious child's house to play, something new is being introduced into the environment. Some children just don't know how to entertain others. I suggest that parents help their anxious child plan ahead for activities like making cookies or going to the zoo or watching a video. Also shorten play times to a couple of hours instead of an entire afternoon or overnight. These simple efforts can set up anxious children for success rather than failure.

I've noticed there's some sort of unwritten law of parenting which states that when the child's friend shows up to play, the parent walks out of the room. With anxious children, though, it's much better if Mom or Dad sticks around to monitor play and to give their anxious child an idea for a new game or activity if one falls flat.

You can't force success. If playtime is going poorly, cut it short and suggest trying again another day. This can often be the case when the mothers are friends and the children are not. Admit it when you see that your best friend's child and your own child bring out the worst in each other, and don't try to bring them along when you and your friend want to be together.

Play is not always easy for children, especially anxious children. Parents have a normal expectation that all children love to play and, therefore, that all children have a talent for it. But some children don't know how to play. When this is the case, play, which should be an anxiety reliever, can become an anxiety producer.

Parents who pick out toys for their children based upon what other mothers say their children enjoy or based on television commercials may have a rude awakening when their child rejects a new toy. Too often the problem is that instead of playing with children, we give them things to play with. I try to encourage parents to show their children how to play with new toys by joining them in the activity. You can buy your little girl a dollhouse and it may sit untouched for months. But if you sit down with her and become involved yourself, you can begin to open up her imagination and spur creativity.

Because of the nature of my practice, I spend time playing with lots of different kids. It is amazing to me how different their styles of play are. I see how play works as an anxiety reliever because in play, a child can be in complete control of the situation. Kids will try on different personalities and situations.

They will work out problems. But often they need guidance to get started.

HELPING THE ANXIOUS CHILD
THRIVE IN SCHOOL

To help an anxious child thrive in school, it is important to remember that teachers have personalities, too. Teachers' expectations affect children just as parents' expectations do. If your anxious child is made more anxious by a teacher who is not understanding of the child's temperament, then it may be best to try another teacher.

Consider what makes an anxious child more anxious—loud voices, flaring tempers, unexpected events. If your anxious child has a teacher who is loud and gets upset easily and has an affection for pop quizzes, your child is probably not going to thrive in that particular classroom. However, put the same child in a classroom with a teacher who has a soft voice and a calm demeanor, who knows not to call on your child unless his hand is already in the air, who is helpful and supportive, and your child is going to do far better.

I suggest that parents of naturally anxious children have a meeting with their child's teacher early on in the year to explain his temperament, make some suggestions for dealing with it, and gauge how helpful and cooperative the teacher is going to be. I find that many parents are afraid that if they talk to their child's teacher, or if the teacher is uncooperative, talk to the principal, their child will be labeled a problem child. But there are ways to get around this successfully.

Don't use the word "anxious," for instance, but describe your child as "shy" or "slow to warm up." Explain that your child works hard and often knows the answer, but will panic if called on in class. When talking to the principal, use positive phrasing such as, "I know you understand children like this probably better than we do, and I trust that you'll place my child with the right teacher who will understand him." Although schmoozing teachers and principals may seem manipulative, I find it usually works and works well.

If your pleas with teacher or principal fall on deaf ears, don't wait too long before looking elsewhere for intervention. Talk to a counselor, a pediatrician, or a psychologist and get them to intervene as a higher authority. It often takes a professional to make an impact in a difficult situation. The wrong teacher can do real damage to an anxious child, damage that will take a long time to undo. When your child comes home crying from school, listen and learn. I once had a case where it took nine months to undo what one wrong teacher did to a child in only the first few months of the school year. Note that I didn't say "bad" teacher, but "wrong" teacher. A demanding teacher who uses language such as "A child in my class *should* be able to do such and such and *will* do such and such when I say so" may have excellent influence on the low achiever who needs an extra-hard push, but can do real damage to the shy, anxious child. Don't place your child in a no-win situation.

If your child comes home from school crying because the teacher embarrassed him, try the following. Make an appointment with the teacher at a nonembarrassing time for your child, before or after school, and take your child with you for the appointment. You don't want to exclude the child from the situation because, after all, this is about his behavior. If you go to school alone, you risk slipping into a rescue mode. Talk to the teacher about your concerns in a positive way geared to preventing this embarrassing situation from happening again.

If your child protests to the extreme, say, "Okay, I won't talk to your teacher now, but if things don't get any better, I'll have to. I care about you, and I can't watch you feel this way. I'll abide by your wishes to a point, but I am not going to let anybody continue to do this to you." It's very important in this type of situation for your child to know that you're on his side. Consider the following situation. A second-grade teacher embarrassed a child in front of the classroom because she read an answer incorrectly. The little girl began to withdraw and finally refused to participate. The teacher began to send notes home about the lack of participation, so the pressure only increased for the little girl to participate. The longer it continued, the worse she felt.

Finally, the child didn't want to go to school and began to show anger at home. The root of her anger was that she expected her parents to take care of her, to defend her with the teacher. In this situation, I intervened with the teacher on behalf of the parents and the child. I explained what the child's perception of the embarrassing situation was, and that whether it happened exactly that way or not, or whether it was intentional on the teacher's part or not, it was causing serious problems for the child.

I asked the teacher to help the child if the answer came out wrong rather than correcting her in a way that the girl found embarrassing. That way, the girl would be encouraged to raise her hand. The teacher did cooperate, and I also consulted with the third-grade teacher through the next school year. Meanwhile, I talked with the little girl about the subjects she knew well and encouraged her to begin to participate in a subject where she had a degree of confidence. We went over reminders such as "Be sure you're on the right page" or "Be sure to be listening carefully" or "Be sure your homework is in the right folder," so she wouldn't be caught off guard. We began to build a checklist starting with just a few reminders and building on them until she became confident that she was prepared each day.

NURTURING THE ANXIOUS CHILD

Kids, anxious or not, will usually try to act the way they think their parents want them to act—at least until they are adolescents. So, if a parent wants a child to act in a way that is very different from that child's natural temperament, it will either make the child angry, because you are trying to make him (or her) something he is not, or it will make him panic because he doesn't feel capable of doing what you want him to do. There is a trick to influencing the anxious child. While you can't make a passive child aggressive, you *can* teach a passive child how to handle aggressive situations.

Following are some simple steps toward successfully nurturing an anxious child:

1. Stop and evaluate when your child bucks your system. Look and listen for the temperament of your child.

2. Don't forget, your child is not "doing this to you." He probably inherited this temperament from you.

3. Don't try to change the temperament of your child because of the hurts you suffered as a child for having the same anxious feelings. If your child is shy as you once were, you can't talk your child into becoming an extrovert.

4. Don't place your child in situations that are contrary to his temperament.

5. Identify potentially traumatic situations that may cause anxious feelings and talk about them ahead of time and often. As children grow, their brains are constantly evolving. They will look at problems differently at each developmental stage.

6. Encourage children to make mistakes, to try, and if they fail, to continue.

7. React appropriately to situations. Don't scream over spilled milk. Save your extreme feelings for the big stuff.

8. Set limits for teasing in your family. Making fun of faults can induce greater anxiety in an anxious child and negatively affect self-concept and self-esteem. Encourage all family members to laugh at themselves and their shortcomings. It is far better to laugh at yourself than to be laughed at. But don't allow aggressive family members to try to tease an anxious child out of his shell.

9. Avoid using the following words with anxious children:
   • need to

- ought to
- should
- must
- have to
- got to

10. Be more positive in your words choices. Find alternatives to the following words:
    - no
    - not
    - quit
    - stop
    - don't

11. Ease your anxious child into activities through family involvement. Join a youth group or volunteer as a family. Attend events on a regular basis with other families who have children of similar ages.

3

Anxiety and Your Child's Health
RECOGNIZING PHYSICAL PROBLEMS

Anxiety is not a problem that is "all in your head." How we feel, our fears, our anxieties affect our physical health just as our physical health affects how we feel emotionally. The physical and the emotional maintain a close dance that undergoes many twists, turns, and fast steps. When we have problems, it's the job of doctors and therapists to decipher this constant tango, figure out where the problem lies, and then treat it to the best of their abilities.

Exploring symptoms of anxiety with children, especially very young children, is a challenge. By the time most children are eight years old, they should be able to express how they feel—whether they're worried, anxious, scared. But before eight, it's hard to diagnose children for anxiety because of their inability to express themselves in emotional terms. Doctors, therefore, rely on many other clues—antsiness, for instance, which can be a symptom of attention-deficit-hyperactivity disorder, or an anxiety disorder, or any number of physical problems. Other easily misunderstood behavioral clues to anxiety are nail biting, a nervous giggle, trouble sleeping, and being quick to anger.

When their children express fear or reluctance to go to school (which can be a tip-off for performance anxiety), parents sometimes jump to the conclusion that their children are simply trying to get out of going to school by crying wolf. The message I try to get across to parents is that we need to take these expressions of fear seriously and make sure they are, first, not a symptom of a physical problem, and, second, not symptoms of a building or serious anxiety disorder. Most of the physical problems discussed in this chapter are rare ones; still, it's important to screen for them.

This chapter concentrates on the physical realm of anxiety including a laundry list of physical problems often misdiagnosed as anxiety as well as some physical health problems that are either caused by or worsened by anxiety. This chapter will also address medicating your child for anxiety problems, and how parents can work with their doctors for the best results.

SIGNS AND SYMPTOMS OF ANXIETY

Following are the common signs and symptoms of anxiety in children identified in the textbook, *Child and Adolescent Psychiatry*, edited by Melvin Lewis.

Physical

Cardiovascular—rapid or irregular heartbeat, flushing, or pallor

Respiratory—shortness of breath, increased respiratory rate

Skin—a blotching "rash," variations in skin temperature, increased perspiration, a burning or prickling sensation

Musculoskeletal—tremor, general shakiness, muscle tension, muscle cramps

Gastrointestinal—diarrhea, nausea, abdominal pain

Other physical symptoms—headache, chest pain, overalertness, edginess, sleeplessness, nightmares, dizziness, fainting, frequent urination

Psychological

Feeling scared, tense, nervous, upset, stressed, fretful, restless

Feeling panicked; feeling like dying

Can't think

Described by teachers or other caretakers as nervous or high strung

Having nightmares or scary fantasies

Feeling different or left out

Behavior is clingy, needy, or dependent

Shy, withdrawn, or generally uneasy in social situations

Underreacts or overreacts

May be reluctant to engage in activities with any possible danger such as climbing a tree or riding a bike

May take excessive risks

PHYSICAL CONDITIONS MISTAKEN
FOR ANXIETY

Allergies

While allergies themselves are not mistaken for anxiety, there is a risk for children with allergies to be misdiagnosed as having anxiety. Allergies can prevent a child from getting a good night's sleep, so the next day, they may be irritable and agitated and exhibit anxious behavior that will lead parents or teachers to believe the child may have an anxiety problem.

Diabetes

Children with diabetes can have the same symptoms as those with low blood sugar—a general anxious feeling, light-headedness, ringing in the ears, upset or queasy stomach. However, the single symptom most indicative of diabetes is an abnormal thirst. Diabetes can also be detected in your pediatrician's office with a blood test and urinalysis. Diabetics have high blood sugar or hyperglycemia and sugar in the urine.

Headaches

Children who have headaches on a regular basis should also be checked out for physical problems including migraine headaches, brain tumors, or the need for eyeglasses. If there is no physical problem identified, a therapist can then address what psychological precipitants might be associated with the headache and work with the child to reassess those thoughts and feelings. Then a therapist can show the child that by taking a walk, riding a bike, or doing something fun, he can learn to cope with those feelings rather than becoming incapacitated by a headache.

Heart Conditions

Any time your child has a persistent racing, pounding, or irregular heartbeat, tiredness or shortness of breath, it's worth checking out with a doctor. Although tachyacardia and irregular heartbeat are signs of anxiety, they can also be indicative of a congenital heart problem that will need specialized medical attention.

Low Blood Sugar

There's been a good deal of debate about the relationship between low blood sugar and anxiety. Two often cited studies, both conducted in the 1950s, are a prime example. The first, conducted by J. W. Conn and H. S. Seltzer in 1955, contended that low blood sugar, or hypoglycemia, was caused by anxiety. During the same year, another researcher, M. Fabrykant, asserted that the symptoms of anxiety are a result of the low blood sugar.[1] This decades-old debate continues today with various studies supporting both sides of the argument. Regardless of which position is right, in my experience, when a child who is hypoglycemic is treated—a fairly simple process that involves monitoring and scheduling meals—the symptoms of anxiety will very often completely disappear.

It's easy to see why many practitioners might guess that a hypoglycemic child has an anxiety disorder since the symptoms are so similar. These children will feel generally nervous and uneasy, will be light-headed, may have ringing in their ears and butterflies in their stomachs.

Determining whether your child has hypoglycemia involves only a simple trip to the doctor's office for a blood test. If your child's blood glucose level is below 50 mg/ml, then your doctor will likely prescribe some dietary changes. Hypoglycemia usually is caused by the body's tendency to over-secrete insulin. This insulin overdose will often produce symptoms of anxiety as well as irritability, anger, confusion and, in some extreme cases, hallucinations.

For children who suffer from low blood sugar, the solution is not found in a sugary kids' breakfast cereal. Quite the opposite. Low sugar meals and snacks are prescribed to keep blood-sugar levels constant throughout the day. Cheese is an especially good snack to restore insulin levels to normal, and, luckily, is also a snack that many children enjoy.

One little girl in the fourth grade was brought to me because her parents were afraid she had attention-deficit-hyperactivity disorder. She was quite bright, but she became so anxious at school that she would not eat lunch because of her apprehension. By the afternoon, she was a bundle of nerves, complained of headaches, and would become shaky all over. She would go home from school each day and stuff herself on snacks. She would eat again at dinner and then go to bed early complaining of exhaustion. The next morning, she would be irritable and anxious again. I requested that the parents get a medical work-up and my suspicions were warranted—she was hypoglycemic. After that, she was instructed to eat snacks in the morning and never to skip lunch. Another snack in the afternoon and a good dinner kept her symptom-free.

Many children miss meals, don't eat the school lunch, and eat too many sugary snacks. But poor eating alone won't *make* them chronically hypoglycemic. This is a medical condition that occurs in about two to three patients per a thousand live births, and there is as much as a twenty times greater risk for low birthweight babies.[2]

Pheochromocytoma

Pheochromocytoma is a very rare condition in which a tumor produces an excessive amount of the hormone found in the adrenal gland. The condition causes symptoms of anxiety along with hypertension. In one case of pheochromocytoma, a child was brought to the hospital and initially thought to be anxious. He also had significant hypertension and this was thought to be from the anxiety. He was flushed, sweating, had palpitations, nervousness—many of the symptoms associated with an anxiety attack. But after a complicated laboratory test screening for this disorder, he was in fact diagnosed with such a tumor. This is a very rare condition, but again, is worth screening for.

Seizure Disorder

There are some unusual seizure disorders that mimic panic attack. In one such case, a young boy underwent outpatient psychiatric treatment for several months and did not respond either to therapy or medication. During the course of reassessing, his doctor ordered an electroencephalogram, which measures electrical patterns in the brain. The EEG was abnormal and indicated seizure disorder. The child was then treated with anticonvulsant medication and the seizures, once thought to be panic attacks, stopped.

Side Effects From Medication

A number of over-the-counter and prescription medications for colds, allergies, and asthma produce anxious behavior in kids. If the anxious behavior disappears, when the medication has run its course, you can probably write off your child's behavior to the medication's side effects. If the anxious behavior persists, seek professional assistance to find the true cause.

Thyroid Disorder

Hyperthyroidism, or an excessive secretion of the thyroid hormone, produces anxiety-like symptoms. This rare disorder, also called Graves' disease, was widely publicized when it was learned that former First Lady Barbara Bush suffered from it. The anxious behavior produced by the disease is virtually the same as that of anxiety disorder. A blood test, though, can quickly determine whether the thyroid hormone level is normal or excessive.

Toxic States

Toxic conditions can produce anxiety-like symptoms. Kidney malfunction can result in toxemia and should be screened for when anxious behavior becomes a problem. On a less serious level, ingestion of too much caffeine can result in a toxic condition. If your child overdoses on colas, anxious symptoms will be a part of the fallout.

Ulcers

Stomach complaints are common for kids with anxiety disorders, but that extra rumbly or hurting tummy could also be an ulcer that is independent of anxiety. Your pediatrician is equipped to determine whether your child has ulcers or whether you should seek psychological counseling for your child to ease the pain. Recent investigations who studied young patients with ulcerative colitis, commonly called Crohn's Disease, have concluded that there is little or no casual relationships between the patients' personality and the disease.

ANXIETY AND OTHER PSYCHOLOGICAL DISORDERS

Depression

Children who suffer from anxiety are usually very controlled in the classroom. They rarely get in trouble for misbehaving or forgetting homework because they are constantly worried about being embarrassed in class. As they get older and school work increases in quantity and difficulty, they still have a need to continue to produce at the same level they always have, so their anxiety heightens. Their increased worry can often interfere with their ability to score high on tests and do their work well. Next, they begin to get behind, their grades drop, and they become even more anxious and upset. Finally, they become depressed.

Most children who suffer from performance anxiety go unnoticed and untreated. Because their anxiety is internal, spurring them on to greater and greater effort, they are not seen as being plagued by anxiety but as being motivated and responsible. The depression, however, is obvious because its signs are external. Often, a child will be treated for the depression, but depression medication does nothing for the underlying anxiety. When the depression goes away, the anxiety is still there, so the child is at risk for the cycle to begin again.

In some cases, anxiety and depression can be treated successfully at the same time with a combination of medications. In other cases, if the anxiety is treated successfully, the depression will also go away. In still others, if the depression is severe, it must be dealt with first before the anxiety can be treated.

Hair-Pulling

Pathologic hair-pulling, or trichotillomania, is actually considered an impulse control disorder, but it is closely associated with generalized anxiety disorder and is also exacerbated by anxiety. We still don't fully understand what causes hair-pulling. We now believe, however, that it is far more common among children than was once thought. There are two types of hair-pullers. The first, sometimes called "baby trichs," is the less serious type, with the behavior usually beginning between one and six years of age and subsiding as a child grows up. Two important studies have associated this type of hair-pulling with both learning problems and iron deficiency.[3] The second type of hair-pulling begins in adolescence and can occur along with a host of serious psychological disorders. With hair-pulling, a child feels an inner anxiousness that begs for a release. That release occurs when they pull out their hair. Hair-pulling can be severely disfiguring; it can leave patients not only bald and without eyebrows or eyelashes but with lasting psychological scars on their self-esteem. Another symptom common among hair-pullers is rapid speech, which is another manifestation of anxiety and the rapid thinking that goes along with it.

The good news is that an aggressive program of medication and psychological counseling can be very effective in stopping this damaging behavior.

One patient of mine began to pull out her hair when she was about one and a half years old, making large bald spots on the side and back of her head. This child had always had an anxious personality. She was a colicky baby who was very sensitive to noise. She could nurse for only a few minutes before becoming tense and fussy. She would twist her hair and pull out big chunks with one hand while sucking the thumb of her other hand. At an even younger age, as soon as her hair was long enough to grab, this child would hold a strand and rub it constantly between her thumb and finger. While cuddling with her mother, she would also try to pull out her mother's hair.

The pulling behavior with this child was sporadic—it came and went with the seasons. In the spring and fall she would pull, but summer and winter she did not. To try to stop the pulling, her parents shaved her head, and she seemed much happier when she had no hair to pull.

We tried behavior modification and created a fairly strict routine for her. She initially seemed happier with more structure in her life. Her parents put a cap on her head at night, and when they caught her pulling, I instructed them to calmly go to her and put her hand down. We had her brush her mother's hair and her own hair and talked about how pretty she was. We also used rewards for the time she was able to go without pulling.

Now in the second grade, her pulling has subsided with the help of therapy and medication, although other non-harmful symptoms of her general anxiousness remain. She is still what I'd describe as an antsy child, but her thirst for learning seems to have replaced her desire to pull hair as an anxiety reliever.

She has had occasional relapses during stressful times in her home when there is a lot of activity—Christmas, Mother's Day, whenever a house full of company is expected. Because of that, her parents try to be very low key about special events and celebrate without the incredible amount of hype that goes on in most households.

I had another patient, a little boy in the fourth grade who also pulled out his eyebrows and eyelashes (pulling out the eyelashes is particularly sad because they won't grow back). In addition to his doctor prescribing medication for him, I taught him relaxation techniques and how to become aware of his habit. We came up with things he could do to make sure his hands were occupied. If this was a behavior that he fell into while watching TV, for instance, he learned to sit on his hands.

I also encouraged his parents to create a calmer household environment and to avoid overloading him with activities in order to decrease the level of stress in his world.

Learning Differences

Anxiety can also be misconstrued as a learning difference, most notably attention-deficit-hyperactivity disorder or ADHD. ADHD has some symptoms similar to anxiety disorder. Children who are anxious will often have trouble performing in school; they may be disorganized and distracted. These behaviors are similar to some of those exhibited by kids with ADHD. However, the cause of these behaviors in anxious children is very different.

Anxious children may be so concerned about performance that they seem distracted because they are constantly going over questions in their head: Do I have everything I need for this class? What's coming next? Did I study what I needed to study? Did I understand what the teacher just said? What if I can't remember the important facts in the lesson?

Because of this constant internal questioning, they miss out on much of what is said in class. One interesting clue to determining whether this behavior is from anxiety or ADHD involves the knowledge of trivia. Overanxious children usually score very low on the trivia sections of intelligence tests. They haven't had time to notice or learn trivia because they are constantly worrying and don't hear these incidental facts in class or in conversations. Kids with ADHD, however, may have very high trivia scores since trivia is often learned through games and short lessons where they excel. A true ADHD child is not a worrier and lets past problems fade. ADHD kids live for today and tomorrow, while an anxious child focuses on yesterday.

In order to be really sure whether your child has a learning difference or an anxiety disorder, have a thorough educational evaluation. The symptoms can be confusing because we're simply not used to asking children about their feelings. With children, we're too often focused on behavior rather than feelings.

Tourette's Syndrome

Anxiety or symptoms of anxiety often are present along with other psychiatric disorders, and doctors and parents must be careful to look past the anxiety to what may be an underlying or more serious problem. Tourette's Syndrome is a disorder often accompanied by anxiety. Tourette's, once considered rare, is now thought to occur in one to ten per one thousand people. Tourette's Syndrome is characterized by physical and vocal tics that come and go. Tics can also be associated with anxiety problems, so doctors must be careful to determine whether anxiety is just a symptom of Tourette's or is itself the predominant disorder.[4]

PHYSICAL CONDITIONS CAUSED OR EXACERBATED BY ANXIETY

Arthritis

Juvenile rheumatoid arthritis and other conditions that involve extreme pain can be exacerbated by anxiety. When children become fearful, a neurotransmitter is released that can make them more aware of or increase their feeling of pain.

For many years, I treated a little girl who had juvenile rheumatoid arthritis and an anxious personality. When she became upset and worried, her arthritis would flare up and she would have to increase her medication and the frequency of her doctor visits, which only added to her fears and worries. This vicious cycle was slowed with the use of relaxation techniques. We also worked with her teachers to create a highly supportive environment for her at school and ease anxiety about performance there.

Asthma

Studies have indicated that as many as a quarter to a third of the children with asthma have attacks that are precipitated by such emotions as excitement, fear, anger, and frustration. Just as some asthmatic children must limit physical activity that can trigger attacks, children who have a tendency to be overanxious must learn to control their emotions.

Heart

Children who suffer from heart defects that produce tachyacardia or rapid heartbeat may also find that anxiety can trigger tachyacardic episodes. At the onset of an episode, children may become fearful and feel out of control, leading to panic, which can lengthen or worsen the episode. Relaxation techniques can be very helpful in these cases, along with teaching children to distract themselves from the pain or discomfort. It's important to make sure the child understands what's happening to his body to lessen the fear factor.

Irritable Bowel Syndrome

Irritable bowel syndrome is another physical malady that, coupled with anxiety, can lead to a vicious cycle. Children with this syndrome suffer pain and excessive diarrhea because of a malfunction of the bowel. One bright little ten-year-old girl with irritable bowel syndrome suffered episodes at school that were triggered by her fear of being called on or embarrassed in class. If she had an episode at school, she would be so worried about it happening again the next day that she wouldn't get a good night's sleep. The next day, she would either miss school or be so tired and fearful at school that she would be called on, not know an answer, and have another attack. After missing school, she was behind, which also increased her anxiety.

In her case, her physical problem was the source of her anxiety and her anxiety triggered her physical problem. Part of the solution was to be completely prepared for school. We set up a checklist so that she was sure she took home the right assignments. We asked her teacher to check that her assignments were written down and that she had her books with her when she left school. We also encouraged her teacher not to call on her unless her hand was raised. She was also given permission to go to the bathroom at any time without asking. Through these efforts, we built up her confidence and eased her fear of being embarrassed. It took nearly a full school year to stop the cycle and help her feel in control.

Stuttering

I once had a professor who said he could make anyone stutter by mimicking them and by calling attention to small hesitations we all make. This type of intimidation is an illustration of what happens to children who are fearful and intimidated by life. Most often I see stuttering with children who have demanding fathers with loud and deep voices that come across in a challenging manner.

When children feel challenged to explain themselves, especially at a young age, it's hard for them to express themselves. When they are rushed and fearful, as the professor made people feel in that class I took, stuttering is a natural reaction. Once they begin to stutter, they're afraid they can't stop and their increasing embarrassment only makes the problem worse.

The number of people who can perform well in front of a group is very limited. In the classroom, when children first begin to read to the class, many of them are intimidated. This is naturally a very anxiety-producing situation. But for the child who stammers or stutters, this kind of situation is almost intolerable. At the same time, to be left out because you stutter is just as glaring and obvious and can cause anxiety, too.

In addition to psychological counseling to find out what is behind the stuttering, I refer my young patients to a speech pathologist to get them past this painful stage. There are many reasons for stuttering. Kids who are naturally anxious are prone to stuttering as well as kids who have ADHD, since they typically speak very rapidly. Others start stuttering when something traumatic happens to them. Also, children with oral expression problems can be candidates for stuttering. (For more information on stuttering due to trauma, see Chapter 6.)

About one percent of all people stutter, but a higher percentage of children will suffer temporary bouts with stuttering. Also, three to four times as many boys will stutter as girls. Between the ages of three and six, children will speak with some hesitations and repetitions. This is natural since their language skills are typically more developed than their articulation skills, which are fine motor skills. In other words, their minds can naturally work faster than their lips at this age. Stuttering acts as a place holder until they come up with the word they want to use.

These natural hesitations and repetitions can turn into stuttering when listeners react improperly. If parents and grandparents overreact and call attention to the stuttering and put a label on it, it can exacerbate the problem. Usually, a child of this age hasn't even noticed the hesitations. When parents call attention to how a child talks, then the child begins to anticipate problems with difficult words. Once that anticipation begins, it triggers a physical response. The heart rate speeds up, the vocal chords begin to react to breathing irregularities, the central nervous system kicks in and perspiration begins.

If your child begins to stutter, there are many things you can do to ease him through this stage successfully:

1. *Become a better listener.* Concentrate on how and when you listen to your child. Do you hurry him through sentences? Do you let him finish talking before you start? Do you look at him when you are listening? How do you react when your child interrupts you? What does your child feel most comfortable talking about? What subjects of his are you most interested in?

2. *Change the ways you listen and react.* Experiment with the way you normally listen and react to your child. Give more or less attention. Change the way you react when she interrupts. Listen more intently in situations where you didn't before or less intently in situations where you did.

3. *Look for feelings behind the words.* Try to decipher the feelings behind your child's words. Listen to manner and tone that may be communicating emotional messages. Watch for body language. How does your child talk to other children, to toys or dolls? Compare this to the way your child talks to you and to other adults. Does he seem to be preoccupied with some subjects? This might indicate what he is afraid of.

4. *Show love and attention through listening.* If you practice the above three steps, you should be able to show your child the love and attention she demands even though you have your own responsibilities. Make a point to interrupt your daily tasks to show interest in what your child is saying and doing.

5. *Learn your child's signals for help.* As you become a better listener, try to discern your child's signals that he needs immediate listening attention. These will usually precede a fretful, crying stage. Watch for clues such as facial expressions, posture, withdrawal, unusual loudness, or increased hesitations and repetitions.

6. *Talk with your child, not at him.* It is very natural for parents to talk at their children most of the time. Make an extra effort to change this habit, to talk with your child about issues and involve him in a discussion. If this doesn't come naturally, set up specific times to talk with your child about topics that he is interested in—*not* about his behavior. Ask him what his day was like. Let him ask you about yours. If your child seems uncomfortable, don't force it. Find a topic later that interests him. Don't be judgmental or critical. This type of interaction will create a nurturing environment for your child to talk as fluently as possible.

ANXIETY AND THE DOCTOR'S OFFICE

Children who must undergo repeated medical treatments and visits because of chronic physical problems such as seizures, asthma, crippling arthritis or muscle weakness, cancer, or other serious illnesses, are at risk to develop anxiety. Sometimes this anxiety is from a fear of treatment. (Fear of the doctor, dentist, and medical treatment will be discussed in detail in Chapter 6.) Other times, children fear being away from medical care. This is a serious problem that can keep patients from getting well. These children's anxieties are often warranted—they fear they will get worse, will have a sudden relapse, will die. Sadly, these fears can keep them sick.

During my years as a psychologist on staff at a children's hospital, I often saw this. Just as children were getting to a point of reducing medication or the number of clinical visits, or the number of breathing treatments, they would suddenly develop something—a pain, a cough, an ache—that would prolong their hospital stay. This is a form of separation anxiety in which the patient must carefully be weaned from their beloved, protective medical cocoon.

I once treated just such a patient with hypnosis, a teenage girl who had undergone regular blood treatments since the age of eight. With the improvement of medical treatments for her disorder, she no longer needed the blood treatments, and doctors were able to reduce one of her medications. Still, as a young girl, she had been told that she would never be able to live without her medication. Even though her body was now producing this needed chemical, she was afraid she would die if she stopped taking it. Through biofeedback, hypnosis, and some cognitive approaches which helped her to look at facts and logic, we were ultimately able to build up her confidence and distract her from her body.

MEDICATING YOUR CHILD

When a doctor suggests that medication is warranted to help with your child's anxiety, it's important to be completely informed of the risks and rewards that go with a particular medication. Although there are many types of drugs used for anxiety in adults with great success, there have been only a limited number of studies examining these medications in kids. Parents should ask the doctor to discuss the particular anxiety disorder being treated, what symptoms the medicine is expected to alleviate, and, of course, any side effects that might occur. Following is a helpful checklist to take along to the doctor before your child is put on a program of medication.

1. What is this medication expected to help?
2. What are the side effects, and when might they occur?
3. How long before we should see benefits?

4. What changes should I watch for, and when will these changes occur?

5. Do I need to alter my child's diet while he is on this medicine?

6. What if my child refuses to take this medicine?

7. If I don't see any changes in the time you've indicated for improvement, should I call you or stop the medication?

8. Will this medication interfere with memory or negatively affect performance at school or in sports?

9. If my child and I forget about the medication for a day, what will happen and what should we do?

10. If this medication doesn't work, is there another one to try?

PART II

The Common Varieties of Anxiety

4

Performance Anxiety
CONQUERING YOUR CHILD'S FEAR OF FAILURE

I can closely identify with my young patients who experience performance anxiety. I never raised my hand in elementary school because I was so afraid I'd be wrong and my teacher and classmates would laugh at me. I never asked a question and never volunteered information. I went all the way through school trying to figure out things for myself because I didn't want anyone to know I didn't know all of the answers.

I was afraid to guess or explore—even when I was in graduate school. What if I was wrong? When it was time for my oral exams, I had a true anxiety attack. Even though I knew the material backwards and forward, when I opened my mouth, nonsense came out. I have to commend the director of my committee for being so kind. He stopped the oral test and let me go home to regroup.

I'll never forget the feeling I had that day. It was almost like a multiple personality disorder—I felt apart from my body. I couldn't stop myself from spewing what I knew to be nonsense. Afterward, I went home and cried my heart out. Even though I was in my thirties, I was dealing with the same performance anxiety that had plagued me as a small child.

Although I was an educated adult with experience in my

field, I couldn't assert my opinions strongly in a discussion. If I knew the answer, I'd speak in a timid voice, and if anyone with a strong voice challenged my answer, I was paralyzed to defend it with the facts and figures and experience I knew to be true. Anyone who had an assured presence intimidated me. Arguing was not on my list of abilities. My response to an argument was to be crushed by the opposition. Any challenge made me feel naked—stripped by my challenger.

When someone asked me a question I wasn't prepared to answer, my initial reaction was panic. I viewed my panic in these situations as a lack of intelligence. To give myself time to mull over a question, I'd repeat it, which not only made me appear to be deaf, but was annoying to others.

Years later, I realized that since I was a small child, my father had given me the message, through his style of ridicule and criticism, that I wasn't bright. His constant challenge lead to my fear of failure. Although for the most part I've conquered performance anxiety, to this day I can talk in front of a group of people and appear calm and collected, but will have sweat to my elbows. I am much more comfortable fielding questions rather than making a presentation.

HOW TO RECOGNIZE PERFORMANCE ANXIETY

Performance anxiety is an extreme fear of failure. Most children will express some fear of failure when they first are asked to perform in school, to read in front of the class or do a math problem at the board. But children who suffer from true performance anxiety can't turn off these natural feelings. They are afraid of just being in the classroom. They are afraid that they don't have the right materials, that they haven't done the right homework, and that they won't have the correct answer if they are called on during class.

Children who have performance anxiety feel that to avoid ridicule they have to do everything right all of the time. They may be overly good in the classroom because they don't want to be singled out. They are afraid to do anything that will cause the teacher to call attention to them. When parents tell me that their children are perfectionists, it's a strong clue for me that their children may have performance anxiety, that they're afraid of making mistakes.

Some children have anxiety so severe that they burst into tears when the teacher asks them to read out loud. Some may pretend they haven't heard the teacher and return her request with a blank stare. Still others act dumb as a defense. It's easier for them to say "I don't know" as an automatic response than to run the risk of saying something they think is right but might be wrong.

Kids whose performance anxiety occurs in situations involving soccer or football or other physical sports may be afraid of getting hurt or being dominated by a stronger child. They are afraid the hurt won't stop and that they will be out of control. This in turn will lead not only to physical pain but embarrassment if they scream or cry. Just like performance anxiety in the classroom, they can't turn off their fears. Since their mind is not on the game, they actually are at a greater risk of being hurt. If they are knocked down, even a small scrape will confirm their fears and heighten their anxiety the next time.

BEHAVIORAL CLUES TO PERFORMANCE ANXIETY

Children with performance anxiety will often resist becoming involved in any activities, from school to church to birthday parties. They will come up with a host of delay tactics, most commonly headaches, stomachaches, crying, or temper fits. They may refuse to get out of the car, or they won't leave your side. School can be painful for these children because, especially in the early grades, there are often right and wrong answers—an 'A' is an 'A', 'red' is 'red'—and no in between. The lines are clearly drawn, and children with performance anxiety constantly are afraid that they will land on the wrong side of the line.

In addition to refusing to go to school and getting sick at school, children who suffer from classroom-based performance anxiety will put themselves down and call themselves dumb even when they have made only small errors on schoolwork. Somewhere, these children are getting the message that they need to be perfect to be accepted.

The child with performance anxiety may have a trash can full of papers. Each paper has only a few words written on it and has been wadded up and discarded. If their handwriting isn't perfect, children with performance anxiety won't stop and erase. Instead, they will start over from the beginning since their paper must be perfect. They'll spend hours getting all the way through a paper to avoid having the smudge marks indicative of a mistake. They wouldn't even think about crossing through a word and going on.

While these "perfectionists" will often make good grades, they don't fully experience their achievements, only their failures. They tell themselves they are going to fail, even when they have straight A's. Their natural tendency is to believe that they will do poorly and everyone else in their world will do well. As they grow up, they will try to rationalize their way out of challenges: "I don't know why I have to take geometry to begin with when I don't have to use it in my life" would be a typical lament. Another clue to a child's fear of failure is when he says an activity or subject is "boring," which is often his code word for "difficult."

Birthday parties trigger anxiety because children don't know what to expect. Often parties include games and competitions that are pure hell to the child with performance anxiety. Imagine how such a child views a simple game such as Pin the Tail on the Donkey. First you are singled out from the group, then blindfolded and twirled about until you are disoriented and dizzy. Then you are told to wander around (while a roomful of children and adults laughs at you) trying to pin the tail in the correct place. When you miss, which is the inevitable outcome, someone removes the blindfold and everyone laughs some more, pointing out the hilarity of your mistake. Swinging at a piñata is similarly embarrassing for children with performance anxiety. If they miss, they are chided. If they break the piñata open, everyone else dives for the candy while they are left standing, helpless and blindfolded.

Children who have performance anxiety don't want to try anything because they are afraid of the unknown. If you try to show them something new, they'll protest quickly, "I know, I know, I know," then try to change the subject, so you won't find out that they really don't know.

A TYPICAL CASE OF PERFORMANCE ANXIETY

Karen is a nine-year-old who recently transferred from a small, nurturing private school environment to a larger parochial school. Her new teacher was extremely organized—so organized that she spent the first ten minutes of parents' night explaining how she wanted children in her class to organize their notebooks. Karen's mom came to me because Karen was throwing up before she went to school, sometimes every day. Also, she started coming home from school every day and requesting to take a bath. Since Karen had never had any problems with school before, her mother and father were worried and wanted me to help them explore what the problem might be.

My suspicion was that the structure of the new classroom was somehow prompting anxiety and Karen was reducing that anxiety by coming home and soaking in the tub. Before approaching the teacher and in order to give Karen time to adjust to these demands, I suggested that Karen's mother help her find some alternative ways of relaxing, too, such as stopping by the park to play on the way home from school, chatting with her mom, going for a walk, or riding her bike. She also tried sitting in her favorite chair and listening to soft, relaxing music. I wanted her to have alternative choices not because taking a bath is a bad choice, but because the bath was begining to look like compulsive behavior and that might not always be a practical solution.

Karen's mother also noticed that Karen had begun to rip up her homework papers and break her pencils while she was doing her homework. Karen seemed to have no patience with herself. Her mother said she had become a perfectionist.

I finally suggested that Karen's mother go to school and walk the halls after classes began and listen carefully. It's so hard to know how your child feels in the classroom, since we really don't know what goes on after the bell rings. We can't know how demanding or understanding teachers are from our short conversations at parents' night or the PTA.

Karen's teacher smiled broadly at each child, saying hello in a friendly way as they came into the classroom. But after she closed the door, Karen's mom discovered that Karen's teacher had a temper. She yelled louder and with greater frequency as the day wore on. She pointed out even small mistakes for the whole class to see. While this teaching style may work wonders with children who need strong prompting, for a sensitive child like Karen who was used to a far more nurturing environment, this aggressive style prompted a severe case of performance anxiety. Karen was terrified to fail in front of this teacher, who she knew would yell at her and point out her mistakes to the class.

Karen's mom tried to work with the teacher and explain Karen's temperament and how the teacher's style was affecting her. But in the end, the teacher was unyielding. This was simply a personality conflict, one that was doing much harm to Karen. Finally, the school principal agreed to move Karen to another class with a more understanding teacher.

HOW TO HELP YOUR CHILD OVERCOME
PERFORMANCE ANXIETY

The following steps can help your child overcome performance anxiety and lead an active, healthy life.

1. Encourage Mistakes to Ward Off Fear of Failure.

The best prevention and cure for performance anxiety is to encourage your child to make mistakes from the beginning of life. Parents need to train themselves to respond to their children's efforts rather than their results. Think about an infant learning to crawl. Often parents wait until the baby has moved across the floor to make a big fuss, when the rocking back and forth that precedes crawling is just as important a developmental step.

When that toddler begins to walk, we tend to praise the steps rather than the falls. Falling, getting up, and trying again, however, are the efforts that should be praised equally or even more intensely than the successful steps. Don't forget to praise your child for each effort made to tie that shoe, rather than for the one that ended in a perfect bow. From these early developmental hurdles, parents need to get in the habit of praising the means as well as the end. Rewards should be given for the effort, not simply the outcome.

When you concentrate solely on the finish line, rather than the race, you are giving your child the message that you expect a good finished product and you unwittingly can communicate to your children that their failed tries aren't good enough for you. Fostering these feelings in your children can lead to fear of failure and performance anxiety.

To help parents see their child's point of view, I often ask them which sport they do not play and why. Their reasons for not playing tennis or golf or football are usually the same: they don't feel qualified, or capable, and they don't feel that they will be successful at it. Then I ask them how they would feel if they were put in a situation where they were expected to play that sport. This is how the child with performance anxiety feels about most of his world.

Next I ask parents to think about a scene in a bowling alley. Usually there are people of all shapes and sizes and abilities having a good time. Why? Because they are not afraid of making mistakes. The occasional or frequent gutter ball is expected.

Even though all mommies and daddies make mistakes, kids rarely see their parents' mistakes. Whether you like it or not, your children will often think you are perfect and that they are the only ones facing these embarrassing situations. Unfortunately, it won't help your children for you to spill the milk so that they will see you make a mistake. You can tell them about all of your own growing-up mistakes, but it won't lighten their load if you expect straight A's on their report cards. Also, watch your own tendencies toward "perfectionist" behavior, keeping in mind that your children learn by example. While you are rewarding any attempt toward progress in your child, do the same for yourself.

2. Don't Let *Your* Peer Pressure Breed Anxiety in Your Child.

More and more kids play soccer these days at younger and younger ages. In many communities, there are organized teams for *three year olds*. Parents sign their kids up for soccer without even asking them if they want to play because they want their children to be involved in the activities that everyone else's children are doing. In our transient society, signing Junior up for the soccer team is often an important social step not for the child but for the parents. One of the quickest ways to get involved in a community is through your child's sporting activities, where the overenthusiastic dad who yells from the sidelines may not only be making his own child anxious but others on the team as well. We all know one of these—the dad or mom who runs up and down the soccer field yelling at his own kid, the coach, the officials. Some kids take this pressure just fine, while others, and especially the young ones, need a less competitive, less pressured environment for play.

There are so many sports for kids to be involved in these days that a busy social schedule has developed, flowing from baseball season to soccer season to basketball season with only a few weeks of free time to spare. If your child is not involved, you may find it difficult to find friends who aren't constantly on the way to a game or practice. Parents in these situations may overlook their child's reluctance to participate in view of the overall social picture. Yet, they may be doing damage that will take years to undo by pushing their children into competitive sports before they are ready.

So when is the right time to sign up your children for activities? When they are ready, they'll let you know. Then sign them up and encourage all of their efforts. Goal or no goal, let them know you are proud of them for trying. If you miss a game, don't let your first question be, "Did you win?" Instead ask, "Did you have fun?"

A child may be set up for performance anxiety even before entering grade school if parents overdid it with the "better baby" educational games or spent excessive time trying to make their child use a pencil before that child was ready. A few educational games are good for preschoolers, especially if they are ones your children choose without prompting. But cramming them down their throats, or setting strict times each day when they will work on letters or numbers or flash cards can set them up for performance anxiety from a young age and leave a bad taste in their mouths for academics.

Again, parental peer pressure may be behind this behavior. It is natural for parents to compare their baby's development to that of their friend's baby. Later, performance in preschool may influence which kindergarten the child goes to, and the "right" kindergarten probably has more to do with where parents' friends' kids have gone than with their own child's individual learning style. I've known parents who converted to Catholicism to get their kids into a certain popular parochial school that fed into a prestigious parochial high school. This kind of parental pressure can prompt performance anxiety in children.

Another reality of our day is that the cost of education has increased so much that parents begin putting extra pressure on their kids as early as the sixth and seventh grade to work hard toward that college scholarship. The middle school years, the beginning of adolescence, is an especially difficult time for kids.

But instead of tempering pressure and allowing kids to go through the terrible teens with less scrutiny, parents instead tend to pile it on.

The same pressure to succeed is often applied with kids who are good in sports. I hear parents tell their eight- and nine-year-olds that they need to choose a sport and practice hard to get a college scholarship, when instead, they should be encouraging them to enjoy themselves and try as many new sports as they may want.

Another area of extreme peer pressure for parents is school test scores. Beginning in elementary school, through the SATs, parents are very aware of how their children measure up to their friends. It is important for parents to realize that these tests may or may not have a relationship to how much their children know or understand, nor can such tests predict how well they may do in college or out in the world. Make sure your zealous encouragement, that extra "how to take the test" class, or your insistence that your child take a test again, has your child's best interest at heart rather than your own bragging rights.

3. Work Against Test Anxiety from Its Earliest Stages.

Test anxiety is an extreme form of performance anxiety that blocks a child's ability to remember answers when being tested. When children with test anxiety sit down to take a test, thoughts start rushing through their heads. They begin to worry about what they have forgotten and areas of difficulty that they hope aren't on the test. While the child without test anxiety may be going over what he does know in the minutes before the test is passed out, the child with test anxiety is in a panic about what he does *not* know. As the thoughts speed up, faster and faster, they literally block information that the child does know. The child automatically thinks, "I can't remember, I don't know," no matter what is asked, and finally panics.

In therapy, I use mini practice tests as well as biofeedback to ward off test anxiety. We imagine situations at school that are stressful to the child, then work through them using exercises to reduce stress and anxiety. I teach them to use "positive self-talk," such as, "I know the answers. I am not going to be afraid. I've read the book. I've studied the material. I know this." When they can talk to themselves in this positive way, they can slow down the negative thoughts that block their knowledge and lead to panic.

I also teach kids some test-taking skills, such as going through the test to look for answers that they know immediately and leaving the difficult questions to the end. I teach them to trust their first inclination since anxious children have a tendency to talk themselves out of the correct answers. With older kids, I encourage them to go and talk with the teacher and ask for clarification or direction if they become confused. Most teachers recognize test anxiety in their students and are happy to help in this way or even to test children with severe test anxiety in a way that is less anxiety-producing, such as with a discussion of the material rather than a written test. Then again, some teachers recognize test anxiety in students but feel that the children need to overcome it by themselves without any individual attention. The sad news is, kids won't overcome test anxiety without help. If you were afraid of snakes, you wouldn't start collecting them. The fear of tests is no different. A child is not suddenly going to enjoy something that is feared by repeatedly being subjected to it.

If you don't work on a child's test anxiety when it first starts, it can be extremely difficult to overcome. If you've helped your child study and know she knows the material, and your child comes home with a low grade, don't overlook this important clue. Talk to the teacher immediately and ask if he or she can reevaluate your child orally to determine if test anxiety could be the problem.

Talk to your child about his feelings and thoughts before and during the test. If your child describes the racing negative thoughts indicative of test anxiety ("I don't know the answer. I won't know the answer. I can't remember. I can't think. I've forgotten everything."), or if he has true anxiety attacks with a rapid heartbeat, sweaty palms, light-headedness, etcetera, you may need professional help.

Again, practice tests can help your child get used to testing. Also, a tutor or after-school educational center can help your child with test-taking skills. Relaxation techniques and positive self-talk can also help stop the negative racing thoughts that keep your child from doing well on tests.

4. Intervene on Your Child's Behalf at School.

Adults often try to encourage children to handle their own problems. They rationalize this in their adult minds as not wanting their children to be overly dependent upon them. But when you have a child who suffers from performance anxiety in the classroom, you can't expect that child to take an aggressive stance, approach the teacher, and explain that he becomes anxious when called on and often knows the answer but is afraid of the situation. This is expecting rational, adult behavior from a child who is paralyzed by fear.

Instead, you need to help your child by going to the teacher and talking about the situation. Explain to the teacher that your child is afraid of answering questions out loud in front of the class. Tell the teacher that your child needs some time and nurturing to build up confidence in the classroom. Help the teacher explore other ways to show or test your child's strengths besides reading out loud or coming to the board to do work in front of the whole class, or whatever triggers anxiety in your child. Then explain to your child that the teacher is not going to call on him until he feels more comfortable and wants to participate.

At the elementary level, I've found that teachers will often be very cooperative, but at the middle and high school levels, you may have a harder time convincing the teacher to give your child special attention. It's hard for teachers with large classes of teenagers to give individual attention to students. Seek out extra help from the counselors' office at school or from the principal.

Working together with a principal, teacher, and a therapist

may be the only way to get a child suffering from severe performance anxiety through the school year. I've found, though, that when everyone works together and has the best interest of the child in mind, progress is noticeable early on. Experienced principals and teachers know how crippling performance anxiety can be to a child. With a little tact and persuasion, you can make them valuable members of a team.

5. Help Your Child Prepare for Anxious Situations.

Whether it is school or soccer or a birthday party, work with your child at home to make sure she is prepared for the situation. With school, have a checklist for your child to run through each day to make sure she has homework, pens, paper, pencil, books, and so on ready. If your child has fallen behind, get a tutor to help her catch up to the rest of the class or to prepare for big tests.

Observe soccer or gymnastics with your child, and then let her decide if she wants to participate. On the way to the birthday party, talk about classmates your child knows well who will be there. Offer to stay if your child wants you to, but try to blend into the background.

6. Build Confidence Through Positive Reinforcement.

Look for any signs of improvement and reward them. Also, praise every try, even small ones, in the process of building self-esteem. If you can help your child develop pride, effort will follow. Help him see the quality of his own work by pointing out strengths.

7. Don't Push.

Don't push children into trying something they're afraid of. If you can't expose them to something new through direct participation, then try involving them through books or through observation. Take them to a friend's soccer game. Observe a gymnastics or ballet class. Remember, kids with performance anxiety tend to be more comfortable with individual sports and activities than with team sports or activities because they only have themselves to please or to disappoint. If they fail, they won't be letting an entire team down, and they won't be compared to other kids on the team who are better than they are. Try swimming, golf, or tennis.

8. Don't Delay Homework Time.

Parents of anxious children tend to assume that since school is so stressful for their children, they need a rest or playtime after school and before homework. Wrong. It's much harder for children to switch gears. Most often, it requires too much concentration for anxious children to switch gears twice, so homework is a struggle or is done poorly. It is best to encourage that homework be done immediately after school with a snack break before playtime. This routine is easier since their brain is accustomed to processing information. It is much harder to settle down to work after having a taste of play. The anxious child will also enjoy playtime more when unfinished schoolwork is not hovering in the back of his mind.

9. Discover Your Child's Learning Style for a Better Understanding of Test Scores.

We now know that some kids are primarily auditory learners who learn by hearing about and then talking through a subject, while others tend to be visual learners who need to read, see, and write down facts and ideas to understand and remember them. I hear parents talk about children who studied and knew the material and then came home with a C. In these situations, I'll ask the parents if they talked through the subject matter with their child and if they gave written or oral practice quizzes. Usually, I'll find that this child is an auditory learner, and, unfortunately, most testing in school requires that children read silently to themselves and then write down answers.

If you don't understand how your child learns, your reaction to the situation might be, "Honey, what happened? You knew everything last night," which the anxious child hears as, "You dumb fool, what did you do wrong?" A better reaction to this situation would be, "Honey, I'm still proud of you. I know you knew the material, but the way your teacher tested you was not the best way for you. Would you mind if I talked to her about that?" The more you know about your child's learning style, the less anxious she will feel about failing because your expectations will be reasonable.

10. Don't Make a Fuss Over Reports Cards—Good or Bad.

Parents unknowingly increase performance anxiety in children by putting too much emphasis on report cards. Parents need to remember that these grades belong to their children, not to them. An appropriate response is to ask the child if he is happy with the report card and then talk about anything he would like to change before the next report card. Be sure to praise and encourage him. If kids understand that their parents are more concerned about the effort put forth every day than the grade given at a point in time, it will reduce their anxiety over grades and they will probably relax and do better, not worse. Sometimes grades are codes given by teachers. I know of some teachers who give A's and B's to children whose work is really only average and deserving of a C. The rationale is that the teacher wants to build up the child's confidence.

Paying kids money for A's and B's sends an even worse message by placing the wrong value on a grade. This practice can also create problems between siblings when some kids make better grades than others.

11. Be Available for Help at Study Time.

Parents need to make themselves available for help during homework time rather than sending a child off to her room to study. First of all, there is no guarantee that when your child shuts her door that studying begins. If studying is more interactive, you not only know your child is working, but you learn more about her learning style. If she is just learning to read and is reading a story for comprehension, help her say the words, don't make her painstakingly sound each one out. That only builds her frustration.

12. If You Don't See Improvement After Trying These Steps, Seek Professional Help.

If you don't begin to see even gradual changes in your child after trying to help him with his anxiety, then find a professional counselor. Without early intervention, it can take many months to undo just a few months of harm from an overbearing teacher or coach who may have unwittingly triggered performance anxiety in your child.

Explore medication, relaxation techniques, biofeedback, and other tools for stress reduction.

5

Separation Anxiety
RAISING INDEPENDENT CHILDREN

Anyone who has been to a mall or a department store has seen at least one common display of separation anxiety—the mom with a two-year-old plastered to her right calf. A child suffering from separation anxiety fears being apart from his parents, especially Mom. While most kids will go through a clingy stage, some kids suffer this fear to the extreme and need special attention to help them grow into healthy, independent children.

Determining whether your child is just going through a stage or is truly suffering from a more serious form of separation anxiety involves some exploration. If your child shows excessive and recurring distress when being separated from home, parents, or primary caretaker; expresses worries about harm coming to family members; worries about farfetched events or disasters that will result in separating him from Mom and Dad; refuses to go to school; refuses to be alone in his room or sleep alone, or has nightmares about being separated; and if several of these symptoms last for several months—and if there has been no situational trauma that might be the cause of the behavior—then your child probably has a full-blown case of separation anxiety.

Younger children who suffer from separation anxiety will

71

most commonly exhibit clingy behavior, refuse to sleep alone, or throw a tantrum when parents leave them with a baby-sitter. Older children will refuse to go to school; be afraid to stay at home alone even for brief periods in the daytime; or will refuse to participate in activities with friends, such as sleepovers or birthday parties, where the parent will not be there. These symptoms may come and go, but will be most pronounced when there is some type of change occurring, such as the family's move to a new neighborhood or city; the beginning of the school year; Mom going back to work after having been at home for some time; or a divorce, death, or other trauma.

If you're still unsure whether your child has separation anxiety disorder, use common sense. Ask yourself, "Is my child's behavior interfering with normal development?" and "Are there other children I know who behave this way?" If you can't name several children immediately whose behavior is like your child's, you should probably seek some professional advice. Your child may grow out of these anxious bouts within a matter of months. If, however, the anxious behavior seems here to stay, get some help.

Minor separation difficulties will subside rather quickly. When you take your young child to school for the first day, it's natural for him to cry and be a little afraid. But most children will be quickly distracted by a teacher into an activity. If your child is not distracted and can't tolerate your absence, try to figure out what might be causing the extreme fear.

Run through the following checklist:

1. Has anyone died in your family?
2. Is anyone in your family sick or in the hospital?
3. Have their been any major moves or changes in your family?
4. Have you had a new baby recently?
5. Has there been any kind of trauma or accident that might have made your child afraid?

Once you identify the possible cause, talk about it with your child. Assure your child that he is in safe hands, that no possible harm can come to him, and that you'll be back at a certain time. Don't be late.

Some separation anxiety may be an indication of a healthy attachment to a parent. A 1991 study of ninety-eight mothers and their three-year-old children designed to measure the effects of temperament and attachment security on a child's separation anxiety indicated that children with a healthy attachment to their mothers experienced more anxiety when separated than did other children. The researchers concluded that although anxiety is not necessarily a desirable mood in children, it might also be proof of a healthy mother-child relationship.[1]

It may be some consolation to know that separation anxiety is the most common form of anxiety disorder in children. It is believed to occur in approximately two to four percent of all children and adolescents and accounts for one half of the children seen for mental health treatment of anxiety disorders.[2]

THE TERRIBLE THREES

It's no coincidence that researchers of separation anxiety often chose to observe mothers and three-year-olds. The third year is a critical one in the development of independence. From infancy, children go through stages that range from total dependence to the first stages of independence, which usually begin around age three. When your child feels completely secure, she will venture out into the world, running back to you for a refill of security. After the reassurance that you are there for her, there will be more experimenting with independence. And so your child behaves in this yo-yo way until the cycle is complete. There are certain children who need to complete this cycle of venturing out and coming back for security without interruption. If there is an interruption—if you spend more time away from them due to illness or work or travel, if you have a baby who takes your attention away from your three-year-old, if you divorce or one parent dies—your child may have a difficult time becoming independent and is at risk to develop separation anxiety.

The critical relationship for children with separation anxiety is the mother-child relationship, rather than the father-child relationship. If the mother is emotionally removed from the child for any reason, then the child could have a tough time developing the sense of security that is essential for them to begin the venturing-out cycle. I've seen children who are afraid that something will happen to their mother while they're at school or at a birthday party. I've seen children develop separation anxiety when their mother is going through an ugly divorce. They sense and observe the stress and depression the mother feels and so they become caretakers who cannot leave their mother for even short periods of time.

Perhaps the most frustrating symptom of separation anxiety is the refusal to go to school or preschool. These children are frustrated by their inability to leave their mothers. As they grow up, they are not independent, and they are very unhappy. Their primary conflict is with that person they cannot leave—their mother.

One of the most severe cases I've seen is a seventh-grade girl who has no patience with her mother. The girl is easily irritated and picks constantly at her younger siblings. She is fine with one-on-one, "only child" relationships. But when she has to compete for attention, she "loses it." Through two years of therapy, we have learned that she has never gotten over her mother devoting attention to a younger sibling when she was at that crucial three-year-old stage. When her mother came home from the hospital with the baby, she had to go to her grandmother's house for a few days, and she still resents losing her mother's emotional attention to her younger brother.

Adolescence is another critical period in a child's journey toward independence. Again, children ages twelve through fourteen must have a strong base of security to continue to venture out farther from their parents' protective circle. One example is an eighth-grade boy who is academically successful, has friends, and gets along well with teachers, yet he cries at school over any conflict. He calls his mother from school every day wanting to come home. School itself has become painful for him, not because of problems there, but because he can't stand to be away from his mother. He is having a difficult bout with separation anxiety during a time when he should be enjoying and testing his independence.

A teenage girl who had never been "homesick" before developed a severe case for the first time when she was fourteen while visiting her aunt. Her mother was involved in a serious relationship and was planning to get remarried. The young girl was afraid that their relationship might change and needed to go home for a refill of security just like those three-year-olds do.

Some kids with separation anxiety appear to be overtly confident and strong. These are usually the children who are involved in an unhealthy family situation where they have had to assume the position of caretaker. Their separation problems usually come much later in life, when it is time for them to go to college or move out on their own. They are not able to separate successfully because they do not feel independent; their leadership role has become their source of security and one they cannot give up. I have one young man as a patient who has not been able to complete successfully one semester in college. He had always done well in school, until he had to go away from his family. He was a caretaker. When he was three years old, his mother was put in the hospital and his father sent him and his younger siblings to live with an aunt. There, he assumed the role of caretaker for his siblings absent both the mother and the father.

If gone untreated, separation anxiety is believed to develop into panic disorder and agoraphobia later in life, and can be severely debilitating.

Following are some difficult situations that are common for children with separation anxiety and a guide to help parents and children successfully deal with them.

Helping Out With Sleepovers

Sleepovers are difficult if not impossible for children with separation anxiety. Don't push your child into "toughing out" these situations. Making them do something they're afraid of is not going to make it easier on them the next time. If they have been invited on a sleepover, talk to your children about the invitation. Ask them how they want you to handle it. Do they want you to say that they can stay until 10:00 P.M. but have to come home because you have something planned for early the next morning? Do they want you to say they have other plans? Make sure your children are comfortable with the solution you suggest. Make sure they know it's okay with you that they don't want to stay overnight with a friend, that you understand their needs, and that someday, when they feel differently, that's okay with you, too.

Easing Into Preschool

One of the factors inherent in separation anxiety is children's fear of harm coming to their mothers or a generalized fear that they themselves will be harmed when they're away from their mothers. For this reason, the first time a mother leaves her child alone in a preschool class or at a childcare facility can be a terrifying experience to the child. To reduce the anxiety of the situation, proceed in slow increments. The first day, just visit the preschool and let your child meet the teacher and some of the other kids, especially if there are one or two kids in the class your child already knows. The next week, let your child stay for just a half hour, then pick him up and go for a fun outing, such as ice cream or to play in the park. Slowly lengthen the amount of time your child stays until he is there for the full session. Remember, you need to show your child that you are not putting him in danger and to slowly build up his confidence to ease anxiety. He has to believe that he's in a safe place and that you'll be there, unharmed, to pick him up on time.

Choosing a Baby-Sitter

In today's frightening and violent world, we have to be careful about who we hire to take care of our children. For a child with separation anxiety, choosing the right baby-sitter is especially crucial. The best choice would be someone your child already knows—a member of your extended family, a cousin, a friend's older child your child knows well. If none of those options is possible, involve the baby-sitter you've chosen in several activities with your child before you leave them alone together. The first time, just stay away for a brief period. Make sure your child knows the baby-sitter has the telephone numbers where you're going to be, or better, a beeper number. Reward small successes and build your child's self-confidence. The first few times, come home before your child goes to bed, or let your child stay up late until you come home.

Going to School

With the majority of mothers working, it has become the norm these days for children to attend nursery school. But not every child is ready for school at age three. If you leave your child at nursery school and he spends the day crying or withdrawn and unable to enjoy the activities, reevaluate, talk to the teacher, and think about giving your child more time at home.

By kindergarten, if your child is still behaving the same way when dropped off at school, you may need to seek outside help. Talk to your child. Explain that this is something he needs to do. All of the other five-year-olds are going to kindergarten and he needs to go, too. Talk to his teacher about the problem and enlist her help. Maybe your child can call you from the office for the first few days at a certain time, just to check in. Tell your child that you'll walk him all the way into class for a week and "hand him off" to the teacher. The next week, you'll walk him to the classroom door, then the week after that to the front door of the school. Try to understand that this anxiety is painful for your child. He doesn't want to be this way and is not trying to manipulate you, but is genuinely afraid.

Sleeping in Their Own Bed

Many kids will go through a stage of waking up in the middle of the night and wanting to climb into bed with Mom and Dad. To keep this stage from becoming a full-fledged separation problem, don't give in, but address the problem from day one. I do think that letting your scared child sleep with you can make the problem worse because it reinforces the idea to them that being near you means safety and being away from you increases danger.

To begin the process of getting them back into their own beds, first discuss the issue of safety. Explain that your house is safe, your neighborhood is safe, their room is safe. Show them how to dial 911 so that they'll know how to take care of themselves if something does happen. Tell them that nothing is going to happen, though, because you are there to take care of them. Then tell them it's important that they learn to sleep by themselves and that you are going to help them learn to do it.

I once helped a family whose only child had developed this problem after they remodeled their house. Prior to the remodeling, the child's bedroom was very near the parents' room. But afterward, the master bedroom was on the lower level and the child's room was upstairs. Soon after the renovations were complete, the child began to develop a problem of wanting to sleep with his parents because he felt so far away from them. Every night became a struggle against his fear of being upstairs and alone and being forced to go up to his room. The immediate solution we tried was having him sleep in a sleeping bag in the den until he was ready to attempt sleeping in his room again. As it turned out, the long-term solution was a dog, which became his sleeping buddy and made him feel safe.

If you try the dog solution, take some extra steps to make sure the dog attaches to the child he's going to sleep with instead of to one of the parents or another child in the family. As often as practicable, have the child be the main person to feed the dog and give treats. Also, encourage your child to spend some time every day playing with the dog or brushing it. When the dog first comes to the house, especially if it's a puppy, kennel the dog in the child's room at night, eventually switching from a kennel to a dog bed.

Buying a pet is by no means the only solution. Come up with relaxing going-to-bed rituals. Set the mood in your child's room by playing soft music. Leave a night light or a radio on. Leave the door open. Begin by sitting on your child's bed and stroking his hair or rubbing his back while he goes to sleep. Then wean him by sitting next to his bed and reading to him. Begin to pull your chair closer to the door night by night until finally, you sit outside his room until he falls asleep. Eventually work toward a story and a kiss goodnight and going back to your own room or your nighttime activities.

Reward your child with praise, or with a sticker for each night he doesn't come into your room. Or propose a special night out together when your child has amassed a week of nights sleeping on his own.

Thumb-Sucking, Nail-Biting, and Bed-Wetting

Thumb-sucking, nail-biting, and bed-wetting can all be signs of separation anxiety and each can be dealt with separately while also trying to solve the basic fear of separation. Thumb-sucking and nail-biting can both be calming agents for the child who has separation anxiety. With both of these habits, your child has to be willing to change before much progress can be made. If she is not ready, any attempts to stop the habit will only lead to frustration on everyone's part. Try to get your child to watch other children and point out that she is the only one her age still sucking her thumb. Tell her you love her very much and you don't want her to be teased and called a baby. There are a variety of things you can put on a child's thumb to make it taste bad, but in my experience, these don't work. They all wash off, and sometimes the child will get used to the taste. If she wants to stop the habit but can't, the best solution is to take your child to a dentist and have a "thumb catcher" device put in her mouth that keeps her from sucking.

Rewards are the best way to encourage children to stop biting their nails. The promise of some special activity they enjoy may coax them into wanting to change.

Thumb-sucking and nail-biting are serving some purpose for your child. Try to figure out what that is and offer a less-damaging alternative.

Bed-wetting is usually not a psychological but a biological problem. If, however, your child has been continent for a long time and then begins to wet the bed, anxiety could be part of the problem. You cannot shame a bed wetter out of wetting. You can use motivation and rewards to encourage him to stop.

Tell your child you'll help with this problem and together you can get rid of it by following these steps:

1. Stop all liquids after 6:00 P.M.
2. Limit sugars and especially orange juice after 6:00 P.M.
3. Set an alarm and wake up your child in the middle of the night to see if you can get a habit going.
4. Have your child help you change the sheets.
5. Institute a reward system for dry nights, such as inviting a friend for a sleepover or getting a new sleeping bag.

There are two other options that come with a price tag. Ask your pediatrician about a new medication, an expensive nasal spray that has been virtually 100 percent successful in stopping bed-wetting. Another solution is an alarm pad; that is particularly effective for the child who wets because he is a deep sleeper and is not getting the message to wake up. The pad is placed under the fitted sheet on your child's bed and, at the first sign of wetness, sounds a wake-up alarm. Your pediatrician can tell you where to get this device. It costs around $50.

Bed-wetting can be the result of many things—a child who is still reticent to leave home to start spending the night out, a push for social interaction with his peers that the child is not ready for, or conflict at home or school, just to name a few. But remember to first check out the possibility of physical problems before assuming the problem is psychological.

HOW TO AVOID SEPARATION ANXIETY

Of course the greatest hope is to be the best parents we can be and avoid separation anxiety altogether. The following *do's* and *don'ts* can help you help your child grow into an independent, happy kid.

Don't Push Your Child Away.

Separation anxiety is a fear. You don't want to push your clinging child away because you'll only increase her fear. Hold her closer. Let her sit on your lap. Hold hands. Hug. Do everything you can to make her feel secure.

Do Set Your Child Up for Confidence-Building Successes.

Be observant at playtime and set up short experiences for your three- and four-year-olds. Try one day a week at a day care facility, a babysitter, or a play group. Praise your child for being a big girl or big boy. Praise independence—getting dressed by himself or getting his own box drink out of the refrigerator—with a gold star. Praise him for wanting to go outside and play without your watching, or for venturing into the sandbox at the park to play with some new kids, or for going to the birthday party and being good.

Do Space Your Children Wisely.

It's best not to have a new baby until your present child has made the independent leap. This is the ideal, but not always the reality in families. So if you do have another child sooner rather than later, be aware that your older child may be insecure and may be extremely needful of security from you, which will result in two demands—the baby with its needs and your toddler with his special needs. Hopefully, with that understanding, you'll be able to attach the baby to your hip and provide your toddler with a secure base and the opportunities and the time needed. Be sure you don't blame your being tired or unavailable on the baby. Just say you're tired or busy, not "I have to feed the baby." Try to carve some time out of the day (maybe when your husband gets home from work) to spend alone with your three-year-old.

Don't Force Nursery School.

Your child is not going to be hopelessly behind if nursery school doesn't work. A lot of today's successful people did not attend nursery school. It is far better to let children have another year or two at home if they're not ready than to force them into nursery school and a full-fledged case of separation anxiety that may cause problems for years. Make sure your child is comfortable and confident before you send her off to school. With all of the available educational materials, you can provide your child with many nursery school skills at home. The best experience your child receives at nursery school is social—learning to relate to other children. At the age of two, children do not participate in cooperative play but what is called "parallel play," where they play alongside each other. Try a small play group in your home and the homes of friends to help your child get social interaction.

Don't Push Too Many Activities.

If your child shows any signs of separation anxiety, let him spend time at home with you. Don't push activities such as ballet, tap, soccer, gymnastics, football, and a host of peewee sports upon him. Let him observe a sport or activity before he commits. Wait for him to tell you what he wants to do. Too often I find that parents sign up their children for activities for the wrong reasons. I see one eleven-year-old child of divorced parents whose father is a sports addict. The father signs his son up for every activity because he's trying to spend more time with him and because he's insecure about the relationship. Because of the divorce, the child is having a hard time saying no; he's starting to regress and have separation problems. He feels that he's being taken away from his mother, cries easily, and wants to go home. Unfortunately, the boy's reaction only compounds the father's fear that he's losing his son. The root of the problem is that the father is, in effect, trying to guarantee time with his child. He is looking after his own needs, not the boy's.

Don't Send Your Child Away to "Get Her Used to It."

Don't send your child to camp or Grandma's to "get her used to being away from me." It won't work. You'll only increase the level of anxiety. The analogy I use is, if you're afraid of spiders I will not cure your fear by putting you in a room with a lot of spiders.

I see many kids who refuse to go to camp, but have parents who ship them off believing they need the experience. This seems to be especially true of parents of only children. A few days into camp, one boy called home to Texas from Colorado Springs and told his mom and dad either to leave right now to pick him up at camp or to pick him up at the Broadmoor Hotel. Either way, he was leaving.

School trips are another problem for kids who have trouble separating, because it's so humiliating for them when they get homesick. Parents call me to say their kid has called and wants to come home and my answer is always the same: Go get them. The misery they suffer if you make them stay will only make the problem worse. I've known kids who were so miserable being away form home they misbehaved until they literally got themselves sent home from a school trip.

Do Encourage Relationships With Younger Children.

Often children with performance anxiety will be more comfortable associating with younger children. I encourage these relationships because they are ones where your child will often be successful and gain confidence. Encourage your child to be a tutor for the younger grades at school or to become a helper at Sunday school for the younger grades.

Do Leave Reminders of You With Your Child When You Are Away.

Put a picture of you and your child in her lunch box. Write a note and just say, "I love you." Leave a tape of a favorite song or bedtime story for her to play when you're out for the night or on a trip. If you're called away from home or are on an adult vacation, set up times before you leave to call your child.

Don't Rush Your Child Through Developmental Stages.

Don't rush your child into giving up a security blanket or special pillow. If your schedule is busy, make sure you don't add your own anxiety to your child's. Busy mothers trying to toilet train their children will often try to make them go on the parent's schedule. But if you're in a hurry at potty time, your child will pick up on your sighs and pleas, and chances are he will be unsuccessful. If your child is beginning to show independence by dressing himself, realize that it will take him longer. Don't give up on him and do it for him so that you can make your bus or train. You are interrupting his show of independence, which is important in avoiding separation anxiety. Realize that some children are slow eaters. Don't rush them through breakfast and plant the seeds of anxiety in their day.

Do Be Ready to Parent.

There is far more to parenting than changing diapers and making formula. Be sure you are ready to have children before you have them. I've seen many parents who weren't ready for children and then found the tasks revolving around children's needs frustrating. Children are smart and sense your frustration. They notice a lack of smiles or deep sighs that can set them up for anxiety problems based on their parents' inability to parent.

6

Trauma-Induced Anxiety
WHEN BAD THINGS HAPPEN TO LITTLE PEOPLE

Children face severe, unexpected traumatic events just as adults do, but often, because they are children, we tend to minimize the effect upon them, explaining it away with hopes that they do not fully understand what is going on around them. Also, we consider children to be so resilient that we don't expect them to have the same kind of recall we do. Children's remembrances are often compressed in their brains into general memories, but by asking specific questions, you can get children to recall as well as adults. Children can remember as many details as adults can, or more, and they have the same tendencies to replay frightening events over and over again. And while it may be true that they don't completely understand hurricanes, floods or earthquakes, drive-by shootings or terrorism, that doesn't minimize the fear they experience during the event or the worry, anger, loss, and confusion they feel afterward.

In recent years, psychologists have taken their practices to the streets and schools in the aftermath of disasters and have learned that early intervention is crucial to minimizing the psychological aftereffects of trauma. As a preventive measure, children should receive special psychological attention, since some studies have indicated that children under eleven years of age are three times more likely than adults to develop post-traumatic stress disorder (PTSD) after going through a severe trauma. Other studies have also indicated that children who have problems with anxiety before a traumatic event are more likely than less-anxious children to develop PTSD.[1]

PTSD is characterized by a continued reliving of the traumatic incident. Young children may make a game of the event and play it out over and over again. Others, slightly older, will have a recurring nightmare about the event or suddenly feel as if the event is happening to them all over again in a flashback or hallucination. They'll suffer intense distress when faced with returning to the scene of the event or its anniversary or any kind of reminder. They'll avoid talking about it as well as avoid any activities that make them think about it. They may develop amnesia specific to the event, lose interest in friends and normal activities, feel detached, be unable to express love and affection, and may see themselves without a future, with no college, career, or family life.

They may have persistent symptoms of insomnia, irritability, have difficulty concentrating, be inordinately vigilant or easily startled. And all of these symptoms may have a delayed onset of six months, a year, or more after the initial trauma.

Following are a variety of traumatic situations that children might face and some suggestions for dealing with them that may help prevent PTSD. After any traumatic situation, if your child begins to withdraw from you or is unable to talk about what happened, seek professional help sooner rather than later.

ACTS OF GOD

If you live in a tornado-, hurricane-, flood-, or earthquake-prone area, it is good to have a before, during, and after plan to rely upon in case one of those events actually takes place. If your child is not overanxious or oversensitive, talk about the probability of the event, explaining that you have a safety plan just in case something happens. Run through the safety plan, such as going to the center of the house away from windows for a tornado, or getting outside of a building in an earthquake.

During the event, try to stay calm. Your child will pick up on your anxieties and will be more anxious if you are. I realize that this is easy to say and much harder to do. None of us knows how we will react to a disaster until it hits us. But try to remember that staying calm and acting quickly to protect your family may help to save your lives.

Once you're in a safer place, talk to your child. Let him know that you're all together and you've done everything you can do to protect yourselves. Talk about your feelings—that you know this is uncomfortable and frightening, but that it will soon be over.

Don't let the conversation stray to what could happen. Instead, concentrate on the moment and what you can do to get through it together; try saying a prayer or singing songs or talking about happy times. Make every effort not to lose control.

After the event, spend a lot of time talking about what happened. If your child initially refuses, try talking about it in terms of how you'd feel if you were him, such as: "I don't know about you, but I was scared" or "I bet that was scary for you—I know I was scared." Try to get him to draw pictures about the experience. First ask him to draw pictures of himself during the frightening event and then of himself or the family after the event. It is possible that after talking it through, the child will picture himself as a survivor instead of a victim.

The National Organization for Victim Assistance has come up with three successive steps to working through a trauma.[2] The first, called Safety and Security, involves making the child feel safe and secure from further trauma. You could involve your child in helping families who lost more than you did during the disaster—for example, boarding up windows to make a house safer or gathering supplies for those who suffered heavy losses. Limit television time, since the disaster is likely to be replayed over and over again. This can be especially confusing to small children who may think the hurricane or tornado isn't over yet as they watch it being replayed on television.

The second step is called Ventilate and Validate, and concerns helping your child work through the experience and his feelings including anger, fear, confusion, sadness, grief, and loss. Let your child know these are normal and common—that you feel this way, too, and that you'll work through them together. Talk, talk, and then talk some more.

The last step is called Predict and Prepare, and involves actively preparing for future disasters or for the difficult times that lie ahead as you clean up and rebuild. You might talk about events that could trigger a reliving of the fear of the disaster, such as the anniversary of the event, or hearing the storm siren, or seeing the weatherman on television give a storm warning, or experiencing lightning and thunder. Then talk about how you and your child can keep fears from becoming extreme by being prepared for them and by understanding why you're scared.

If your child's fears become severe or do not subside as the event recedes farther into the past, seek professional help. Take advantage of psychological group services that may be available free of charge from disaster relief organizations, especially during the days and weeks immediately following the event. Everybody will have a hangover from a traumatic act of God, and the intensity of the experience will influence the intensity of the reaction to it. The fears could continue to disturb your child for years if you don't get help.

CRIME

With crime leading the evening news every night, many children are afraid of what might happen to them. Some kids may begin to withdraw from situations they believe are dangerous after witnessing them on television. They may even refuse to leave home or go to school. Unfortunately, you can't honestly tell children that nothing is going to happen to them because the truth is, our streets and cities are dangerous. What you can do, though, if their anxiety becomes crippling, is to help them regain some sense of control.

Teach them how to dial 911, how to use the security system, and how to lock the doors. Let them take karate or other self-defense courses that may ease their anxiety and help them feel more powerful over their environment. Make sure you don't leave them alone or put them in situations where they feel vulnerable. Teach them basic safety about staying in groups at the mall and not staying out after dark. Teach them how to scream—usually not a tough task for small children—and when to scream or run. Get to know your neighbors so that your child will feel comfortable calling for help. All of these tools will help your child feel less anxious about crime in our midst.

One little girl I helped was traumatized after an attempted break-in at her home. Her father was out of town and the six-year-old girl, who was in her bedroom upstairs, heard someone trying to break in downstairs. She alerted her mother, who, after calling 911, herded the whole family into a room to wait for the police. Although the police got there in time and the break-in was stopped before anything happened, the little girl was afraid to go to bed at night for two years afterward. Each night she had to check and recheck to make sure every door was locked and that the alarm system was on and working properly.

Kids who have had experiences with crime in their homes often feel especially vulnerable at night. It is wise, at first, to let them walk around and check the doors and windows and alarm system, or to sit with them while they are getting relaxed and preparing for sleep, or to leave a light on in their room or in the hall. But for this to be necessary two years after the event is not normal.

I talked with this little girl about what was real and what was imaginary. We talked about trusting, and I planted the idea that once she checked the locks and doors, she had to trust that everything was okay. Then we talked about what she knew to be true—that dialing 911 had worked for her. The police got to her house and nothing bad happened. She was afraid more of what could have happened than of something real that did happen. These discussions seemed to give her a feeling of power and control again. After three or four visits, her feelings of anxiety were greatly diminished.

If the child does experience a disaster at home or at school or in the neighborhood, talk about it and talk about it and talk about it. If what happened affected your child's entire class at school or a group of friends, get them together as a group to talk so that they know they're not alone when they have these fearful feelings.

If your child is very young when she's traumatized, be sure to talk about the event from time to time as she grows up. Your child's brain is in a continuous state of maturation, and as she grows up, she will view the situation differently and will gradually understand various concepts from the black and white to the abstract. At each stage of development, your child will have different questions and different fears that need to be addressed.

Remember, if you're not able to reduce your child's anxiety by talking with her, seek out a professional for assistance. You are not inadequate if you make the same comments a professional might make and your child still has trouble. Sometimes, it just takes an outside, impartial source to help your child see her way past the anxiety.

WITNESSING TRAGEDIES

This is another type of trauma where children tend to fear what might happen instead of something that actually did happen. I had one young patient who was three years old when she saw her four-and-a-half-year-old brother drown. Soon afterward, she developed a stuttering problem, but her parents waited several years to get help. By that time, the stuttering and the fear were very hard to break through. The drowning had become a family secret that wasn't talked about. Her fear was that her parents blamed her for the drowning. As this little girl grew up, and her young brain matured, she had many questions about what had happened. But the subject was taboo in her household.

Another child—a second-grade boy I met with a few times—had seen a classmate get hit in the head with a baseball bat. The ambulance came to the school and took his friend away to the hospital. Many of the kids were traumatized, but this child, more seriously disturbed, was unable to go to gym class. I encouraged his mother to talk to the gym teacher and ask if there was another activity other than baseball her son could do for a week or two. He stayed involved by helping to carry equipment and keeping score. The teacher, who was very cooperative, let him know every day that he was missed and that whenever he was ready to play again, he was welcome. After school, his mother would talk to him about how the game went in class and point out that it had been some time since anyone had gotten hurt. Was he ready to try again? With some gentle coaxing, he was soon playing ball again with the rest of the class.

GOING TO THE DENTIST OR DOCTOR

One of the best ways to reduce your child's anxiety about going to the doctor or the dentist is to set up a time to take her in to meet the doctor, dentist, nurse, and technicians, and have a look around before undergoing a quick noninvasive procedure. This way you can familiarize her with the people and surroundings at a time when she doesn't have to stay long, and when she won't experience any discomfort from a shot or a cleaning.

If your child is extremely fearful about going to the dentist, choose a pediatric specialist. He (or she) and his hygienists and assistants will be more understanding and better prepared to help your child through the experience. Often pediatric hygienists will familiarize kids with each piece of equipment, let them use the suction wand themselves, or use it on the hygienist to give the child some control over the environment before they get started on the dental work that needs to be done.

With some kids, it's best to explain what is going to happen at the office beforehand. With others, this does not calm them but makes them more anxious. You know your child best. Use your own judgment about how much to tell and when to tell it.

Minimize the time your child has to wait in the doctor's or dentist's waiting room. If there is a long wait, ask when you should come back and then take your child for a short drive to get ice cream or for a walk in a nearby park. Even though most waiting rooms have toys, books, and games, bring along a few of your child's favorites from home to keep her focused and distracted while she's waiting. Finally, plan a special activity for after the visit such as going to the zoo or to your child's favorite place for lunch. That way, she has something to look forward to and will focus beyond what is going on in the present, which may be unpleasant.

SERIOUS CHILDHOOD ILLNESS

Children who have serious illnesses and must undergo multiple or painful treatments or therapy are at special risk to develop trauma-induced anxiety problems. With many of these patients relaxation, meditation, and hypnosis can be very effective in reducing fears.

I used hypnosis with one eleven-year-old girl who had a rare disease that required her blood to be washed to remove plaque. The process took two and a half to three hours and required a tube to be put in each arm, one for blood coming out and the other for blood going in. Although it was not a terribly painful procedure, it was uncomfortable and required that the girl lay still the entire time. She quickly developed an emotional reaction to the procedure and would do anything to postpone it. Finally, she would begin crying and work herself into a complete panic. I was called in to try to hypnotize her before the tubes were inserted and was able to get her into a deep, relaxed state of hypnosis that lasted throughout the procedure.

Another child who had to get gold shots as treatment for his arthritis would fall apart each time he had to go to his doctor's office. I trained him to relax himself. We would talk about his dreams and talk about relaxing thoughts, and as he calmed down and stayed relaxed, I'd tap his arm as if he were getting shots; this method trained him to stay relaxed when it happened.

With many of these chronically ill children, I try to get them to think of their body as separate from themselves. The shot or dialysis or chemotherapy is something their body needs and is temporary, I explain. When they can separate themselves in this manner, it is easier for them to stay relaxed and calm during procedures.

With kids who have cancer and need procedures like bone marrow transplants, it is usually a good idea to give them as much information as you can about the procedure so that, through knowledge, they can gain a sense of mastery over their fears. Many hospitals have presurgery tours to make a child familiar with the surroundings and procedures of the hospital. A doctor might explain what he or she is going to do by using a child's favorite doll or bear and then let the child perform the procedure himself to make sure he understands.

You can also teach your child how to use guided imagery to distract him from the procedure. Have him imagine a calm, serene, happy situation like being on a beach. Talk about the birds he sees, the waves lapping on the sand, the ocean breeze. Or ask him to imagine a place where he feels safe and secure and happy. Talk about what that place looks, feels, and smells like. Practice "going there," and help him know that he can go there whenever he needs to, such as during an unpleasant medical therapy or treatment, or when he's in pain from the illness.

FAMILY SECRETS

If you have any ongoing trauma in your household, whether it is an alcoholic spouse, an abusive spouse, or a violent teenager, keeping these family secrets can cause much damage to your younger children. When things are not spoken about in families, when there are secrets, kids will get anxious. They may not see or understand the family problems, but they will pick up on your secretive nature, and they will know that means something is wrong.

One three-and-a-half-year-old boy was brought to me because he would only go into two rooms in his house, the den and the kitchen, where he most often found his mother. At daycare, he seemed just fine. After talking to the whole family, I learned that the father was an alcoholic who was prone to explosive rages. Also, the father watched extremely violent shows on television, unaware that his small son was also watching. This influence made the child increasingly fearful until he would only go into the two rooms. The repeated traumas he suffered made him afraid in any other rooms in the house.

Our plan of action first involved explaining to the father the cause and effect of his own behavior. We had to reduce the incidence of trauma and change the home's atmosphere to make the boy feel safe and secure. We also had to bring the problem out in the open so that it was no longer a family secret.

In abusive situations, the family secret often manifests itself in discipline problems with the children. One of the many damaging side effects of an abusive relationship is that when one parent degrades the other parent in front of the child, the submissive parent loses power. He or she loses the ability to discipline or control the child because the power has been taken away by the abusive parent. Usually this forces the submissive parent to overcompensate and become too permissive with the child.

In both of these instances, keeping the trauma a secret is as damaging as the trauma itself. It always amazes me when parents think they can keep secrets from their children. They forget that for two and a half years of their lives children have had to understand language even though they weren't using it. They have had to be very keen to body language to interpret your behavior while they learned more and more words. So, just because you haven't sat down with your child and discussed the problems in your household, don't expect that your child doesn't have surprising insight into what's going on. Every child I treat knows exactly when things aren't going right at home. The danger here is that because young children are in the narcissistic phase of development, they will automatically think that whatever is going on is their fault. This phase lasts until age five or six.

This is particularly true in divorce situations. Children in the narcissistic stage will believe the divorce is due to their misbehaving or poor grades. (Problems associated with divorce will be dealt with in greater detail in Chapter 10.)

Keeping family secrets can also put your child at special risk for sexual abuse. One common approach by perpetrators of this crime is that they will entice youngsters into keeping secrets. Supporting the concept that keeping secrets is okay, therefore, may make your child vulnerable to abuse.

In general, secrets don't bring out positive feelings in anybody. Think back to when you were a child. If you walked into a room and two other kids started whispering, how did you feel? You do need to teach kids to have confidences and to keep confidences, but make sure they know that they can tell you anything—and that you don't keep secrets from each other.

LOSING A PARENT

Losing a parent is the single most traumatic event that can happen to a child. Children can develop speech and behavioral problems as well as numerous learning problems from this trauma. When this tragedy happens to a child, I suggest that parents and other caretakers avoid making up flowery stories to explain that "Mommy has gone to sleep" or "Mommy has gone to live with the angels." These concepts can be confusing to small children, especially as they grow up and begin to understand abstract concepts.

I do recommend buying an age-appropriate book and reading it to your child, but not forcing it upon her when she's not interested. E. B. White's *Charlotte's Web*, a book that deals with death, is perfect for small children. As your child grows up, your explanations can become more sophisticated. There are many books that can help, including those by researcher Elisabeth Kubler-Ross that document near-death experiences.

Kids will often worry about death when they are undergoing change. As they start to expand their horizons and go farther and farther from home, they will worry about their other parent or caretaker dying. The same thing is likely to happen again when they are teenagers and are getting ready to go out into the world. It will help ease their fears to talk about what will happen to them if you die. Let them know that you've made plans so that they will be cared for and safe if something happens to you. Let them know it is okay to have these feelings.

SEXUAL ABUSE

Sexual abuse is a hot issue and one that every parent fears. Whenever I speak to a group of parents, I am inevitably asked about when they should tell their child about "good touch" and "bad touch," and about how to teach their children to be wary of strangers and at the same time keep them from being afraid of the world.

There's no quick and easy answer. I can't just say to begin "good touch" and "bad touch" teaching at age two, because not every two-year-old is ready to hear about this frightening situation. I have had to undo the damage done to many naive, sensitive, trauma-free children from good, loving homes, who have been subject to the good intentions of a "good touch," "bad touch" talk before they were ready to hear it. Often these were programs in preschools or kindergarten that ended up doing more harm than good and severely frightened these children. Some of them had nightmares; others were afraid to go to school or to leave the house.

My advice is to know your child. Know his temperament and level of sensitivity and anxiety. If he is going to be in a situation where he's at risk for abuse—with a baby-sitter you don't know well or in a preschool or daycare center—buy an age-appropriate book about good and bad touch and read it to him. It can be harmful, though, to force the book on him before his ready for it. Don't dwell on the subject out of your own anxiety. Most importantly, know your baby-sitter.

The concept of "stranger" is a difficult one for small children to grasp. We talk about strangers doing bad things to them, but most often the guilty party is not a stranger but rather someone they know, a teacher, coach, family friend, relative. Your children will not recognize these people as strangers, nor will they think anyone who smiles at them is a stranger. What about the mailman and the policeman? They say hello and Mommy is friendly to them. So who is a stranger?

Beginning when they are toddlers, explain it in terms they can understand: "If you do not know their name, and I do not know their name, then come and get me," is a good way to start.

Then you take your child to preschool, where they know the teacher. Is she a stranger? You have to be careful to differentiate it for them: "If I take you someplace to stay, don't worry it's a safe place." But then use your disclaimer: "If anyone, anywhere ever does anything to you that makes you afraid, you need to tell me about it."

Make sure you have an open relationship with your child so that he will feel comfortable telling you anything. "You can tell me all of your secrets and I'll understand." Take the time to have a conversation with your child every day. Ask him about school, his friends, his teachers, what new activity happened that day. "Did you have a good day? Want to tell me about it?"

Because parents are victims of today's frenzied and fast-paced society, they have less time with their children, They often have to take the few moments they have with their children, alone in the car to preach, to pass along some important gem they feel they need to instill. The casualty that results, though, is a lack of real conversation. They don't talk to their children, but *at* them. They have only a few minutes, so they go into their teacher role instead of listening.

So many times, when kids do get a word in edgewise, I hear parents say, "Honey, that's nice, but why didn't you think about so and so. . . . " Parents are too often tempted to throw in some directive that sends two negative messages to their child: one, that the child's choices are always wrong, and two, that the parent is always right.

While parents want their kids to be able to grow up and make good choices, kids need to be able to evaluate a good choice from a bad choice. If parents can't stop preaching, then they send the message to their child that he cannot think for himself because all of his choices are bad. That message is directly contrary to what parents want their child to be able to do.

One way to get out of this preachy mode is to do what I call "playing ridiculous." Instead of coming out and telling your child what he should have done in a certain situation, play ridiculous with it. Talk about all of the actions and reactions that could have happened, let your child fantasize about what he could have done when the teacher blamed him for talking when it was really someone else. "Let's see, what can we do to Miss Jones. We can call up the newspaper and tell them to put it on the front page that Miss Jones made a mistake. Or you could go to the principal and announce it over the P.A. system." Eventually, as the discussion continues, your child will throw out the solution that you think is the best and you can reinforce him on that one. "That would be great. You know, you're right, you should have just gone up and talked to her about it after class. What a smart thing to do." Playing this "game" with your child will help promote the type of relationship where conversation comes easily and your child feels comfortable telling you about all of his problems. This is one of the best ways to reduce the risk of sexual abuse.

I have great sympathy for teachers in this day in age. They are in a very difficult situation. They have to help small children in the bathroom, where many misunderstandings can occur. You have to make it a point to get to know your child's teachers, but at the same time you shouldn't get too close. Don't put the teacher in an awkward situation by asking her to baby-sit. Keep your relationship a working one, not a friendship. This makes it easier to bring up concerns about your child.

It's best to find a school with an ideal student-pupil ratio where teachers work in pairs. This method cuts way down on the risk of abuse, but it's expensive. Consulting with preschools where problems have occurred, I often suggest that parents take volunteer shifts in the school, in classrooms other than their child's, to cut down on risk and to give teachers a needed helping hand. It's a great safety valve.

Realize that this is an issue that teachers are also concerned about. They'll be open to suggestions from parents.

It's so hard to know who to trust with your child. I recommend calling local nursing programs or seminary programs to find baby-sitters. Although agencies go to great lengths to screen out anyone with abusive tendencies, if someone wants to get into an agency for the purpose of abusing children, the sad reality is, they probably can.

It's best to exercise a little paranoia. Make surprise visits home both with new baby-sitters and regular sitters. Do the same at preschool and kindergarten. Call and visit references to make sure they are real. Expect the worst and check it out, then hope for the best.

7

Anxiety and Sibling Rivalry
MANAGING COMPETITION AND CONFLICT

If you have more than one child in your family, you are no doubt familiar with sibling rivalry, competition, and conflict. These are all natural, though uncomfortable, realities of family life. The good news is that with some preparation and appropriate action, parents can prevent everyday minor discord from turning into major anxiety-producing problems for their children.

UNDERSTANDING SIBLING RIVALRY

To some extent, all siblings suffer from performance anxiety in front of their parents. Every child wants to perform well for his parents and needs to feel that his parents are proud of him. If a sibling makes fun of whatever that performance is—telling a joke at the dinner table, playing in a soccer game, playing a board game—the child being made fun of will become anxious. The first feeling that follows will usually be anger, and you'll be called in to referee.

The preventive solution to most sibling rivalries is to make sure that everyone in your family has his own special place, that everyone is praised and known among the other family members for something that is unique to him. You can unknowingly create anxious children who have an exaggerated need to please if you compare them to one another without supporting their differences. Without an equal message of approval from parents, children will develop a fear of falling out of favor that can lead to anxiety.

Tell each one of your children that they have special gifts and then remind them daily by praising them for those gifts. Then it won't matter to Tim if his older brother makes straight A's and he doesn't. Tim's strengths may be at the piano or on the soccer field, and you've made sure he knows that. He'll also be quicker to praise his brother for those good grades if he's confident that you are just as pleased with him for his own achievements.

Kids who are naturally anxious may have more problems with sibling rivalry because they already naturally worry about their own shortcomings. Make sure you let them know that everyone in the family has equal status in your eyes and that you appreciate them just as they are. Mealtime is a great time to talk about what each of your children has done that day and to give everybody time to talk about themselves. If your kids have nothing to contribute about their day in school, don't push, but go ahead and talk about your day and your experiences.

Don't let yourself get caught up in creating the perfect family based on your expectations. If you do, you may become blind to your children's individual strengths. Be careful about heaping your anxieties and expectations onto your children. One of the most common examples of this is the argument over what your child wears. "I can't let my child wear that to school" is a common parental lament in my office. Well, why not? Is what your child wants to wear dangerous to them or other children? Does it really matter? Or are you worried about what other people will think about you because of what kind of T-shirt your child chooses to wear? Just set rules about what is appropriate for the weather. When it gets below 50 degrees, you have to wear long pants and a jacket, for instance. Try not to get too specific about everyday dress choices.

I've had parents worry needlessly about their daughters being too involved in sports because it's "not feminine" or their sons being too involved in music because it's "too feminine." Underneath those worries is often a fear of cultivating homosexual tendencies, which is ridiculous. Studies simply do not support the belief that sports for girls or art classes for boys make them grow up to be homosexuals. When children have talents—whatever those are—they need to be fostered. If your daughter is athletic, encourage her. If your son would rather play the piano than football or would rather work on the computer than be outside, don't worry about it. Don't let your expectations for your children limit them from achieving their goals. Some of the best chefs are men.

To avoid letting sibling rivalry get out of hand, you have to set limits on teasing in your family. A simple rule to follow is that teasing is okay if it is not about shortcomings. In families where everyone appreciates everybody and no one wants to hurt anybody's feelings, you can have fun teasing. But when kids pick on each other, and they don't have an appreciation for one another, they are usually attempting to degrade one another in their parents' eyes in order to elevate their own importance. This is your clue to examine how you are handling your kids. Are you meeting the needs of each one individually? Do they know you appreciate them uniquely? Are the rules in your family fairly applied to each child? Or do you even have clear-cut rules?

When kids degrade each other and tease brutally, I usually find that they feel the family rules are unfair. If "Mom, you never do that to Tommy" is a familiar whine, you can bet that rules in your family are not clearly defined. When your family has a clear set of house rules, and kids know what the consequences of breaking those rules are, then you'll have fewer problems with rivalries.

FOSTERING HEALTHY COMPETITION

Competition between your children is not all bad. Just as anxiety can serve as a motivator, so can competition. But the best competition you can inspire in your children is competition with themselves. Competition is good when winning is not the be-all and end-all, and when you can let other people be better than you are without becoming upset. It's difficult to level the playing field when there are children of different ages playing. Most board games, Monopoly, Clue, or Trivial Pursuit for instance, are unfair when the whole family plays because adults and older children have more knowledge and a greater capacity for logic and planning than do younger children. It's just a fact that the part of the brain that deals with logic and planning is not mature until adolescence. This rule is a good one with physical games, too. Pair up adults with children to make basketball or kickball fair, because the first thing children will do will be to point out the inequities of teams.

If younger children are playing, the best games involve no logic whatsoever. Candyland and Chutes and Ladders are two good ones where the playing ground is fair. Bowling is another activity I suggest for families, because it is one where everybody looks funny and most people aren't that good. A family walk or a picnic are other great activities that are enjoyable and don't have winners and losers. Games like hide-and-go-seek or Sharks and Minnows are other good examples. Even the person who is "it" is having fun and gets to continue playing the game. Charades is fun and noncompetitive. Or have someone read a funny-sounding word out of the dictionary and let everyone make up a definition. The point is to be together, enjoy one another, and laugh—not to win. Remember, good competition in a family means no one is left with a bad taste in his or her mouth.

Volunteer together as a family serving soup at a homeless shelter. Or get involved with a Habitat for Humanity building program. Even the smallest child can plant flowers while older ones hammer nails or mix concrete. Adopt a family at a homeless shelter and involve them in one of your family activities. All of these activities can give you a sense of achievement as a family and bring you closer together without competition that can lead to conflict.

Ideally, you'll reach a point where everyone in your family appreciates each person's accomplishments. Get in the habit of praising efforts. And try to keep family members involved in each other's individual activities. If Susan goes to Tim's soccer games with you, make sure Tim goes to Susan's swim meets. Then you create a family where support is evenly distributed, where everyone gets perks because everyone goes to tournaments and recitals.

This only works if everyone is proud of everyone else in the family. Explain this to young children by using a concept they understand, such as sharing. "You are sharing with your brother by going to his soccer game, and he will share with you later by coming to your meet."

BECOMING A MEDIATOR

Although you can't avoid conflict altogether in a family, you can deal with conflict constructively. Conflict is good only if you are able to reach a resolution. It is very important for parents to teach resolution and to learn how to mediate with their kids to promote resolution. Don't fall into the habit of banishing each child to his room when they argue. This may be an easy way to stop the haggling, but you'll only find the same argument happening over and over again. Work for a fair compromise—"Billy, you play with the video game for ten minutes and then it's your sister's turn." The more you do this, the faster your children will learn to do it themselves.

A lot of a child's behavior is truly based on the expectations of parents. Parents need to be clear about what they expect, and they need to tailor those expectations to each child. Sit down at regular intervals with each of your children and let them know what you expect from them and help them set their own goals. If you boil it down, the basic expectations are really the same for each child:

1. Try your best.
2. Don't be hard on yourself when you make mistakes.
3. Be honest and kind to others.

A good time to do this is in the fall when school begins. The last thought you should leave with your child should be, "I'll do anything and everything I can to make your life happy and easier if you just tell me what you need." I've yet to have a kid take advantage of me when I say that. If I ask them to reinvent the way their house works, the main thing they always want is fairness. If kids feel you're being fair with them, then mediation will take care of itself.

HOW BIRTH ORDER CAN AFFECT FAMILY RELATIONSHIPS

Family planning can make your life run more smoothly. If you have a baby and then another one comes along too soon, problems can arise. A firstborn child who is used to the undivided attention of her mother continues to need that same, soothing, supportive, wonderful response as she ventures out into the world—regardless of the fact that there may be a new baby at home. She is really not ready to leave that security until she is about three. When another child takes the attention or focus away from the older one, the firstborn naturally feels insecure. Suddenly, the mother is not always the same when that oldest child comes back to get her refill of support and safety. This will often result in separation anxiety because you've delayed your child's ability to venture forth. Many eldest children faced with a new baby in the household and not wanting to disappoint you, will do everything they can to appear to be independent, but underneath they are really anxious. Temper tantrums can be a symptom of this growing separation anxiety. Mom is naturally frustrated dealilng with an infant and a toddler. It's easy for her to misinterpret her child's anger as a temper fit instead of an anxious reaction.

Also, if you overindulge your firstborn and then introduce another sibling six or seven years later, your first child will naturally experience a loss of that indulgence, which could result in anxiety. There is a certain degree of satisfaction in being an "only child" because you do get the undivided attention of your parents. You develop a little bit of a "star complex," so the addition of a new star can be devastating. There are several ways these children can react. Sometimes they turn into perfectionists and put intense pressure on themselves to be the best to gain back attention, putting them at risk for performance anxiety. Other times, they become angry and depressed. Remember, they have suffered a loss of the attention that they have counted on for so long.

The size of your family, whether you have one child or ten, is not alone the cause of anxiety in your children. A successful family of any size is one where every child reaches the beginning of independence before another child comes along. This is the ideal. I realize that most families don't actually have their children perfectly spaced three and a half or four years apart. But if you realize that your children are not ideally spaced, you can be alert to the risks and make time to spend with your toddlers to help them over the independence hump.

Learning more about birth order and how it can explain some of your children's behaviors will also help you predict and avoid potential problems. Following is a discussion of the only child, the firstborn child, the middle child, and the last-born child.

The Only Child

Here I speak from firsthand experience, since I'm an only child. One of the most common wishes of an only child is for Mom and Dad to have more kids. Why? Not so much for companionship, but to take the pressure and the focus off of them. When all of your parents' hopes and dreams are tied up in you, it's tough not to be anxious about disappointing them.

The only child is under a lot of pressure. You have to be the son for your dad and the daughter for your mother. Anxiety is often bred in only children because they are overly observed— there is no one else around to share the limelight. Parents of only children also experience anxiety because they are afraid their children won't be well-rounded. They tend to overexpose them to outside people and activities in an effort to make up for the lack of interaction with siblings. As a result, only children don't have much privacy. They are the only one in the house playing music, the only one on the phone, the only one with the television on too loud. There's no one else to draw their parents' attention away from them.

Only children are really a combination of a firstborn and a last-born child. They tend to be perfectionistic like the eldest, because there is far less room to make mistakes. All of their mistakes are seen because they are under a microscope. This can lead to performance anxiety. When parents have more children, they slack off and are naturally not as critical as their family grows. With one child, they tend to be overly critical and overly cautious throughout that child's life.

Like the youngest, the only child is also the baby, protected, coddled. Because of this he or she can have trouble becoming independent and can have problems with separation anxiety.

The Firstborn Child

When a couple's first child is born, they automatically think that child is the center of their world. There are no other children around to distract them from each step of development. They celebrate the first everything, the first babble, the first tooth, the first step. The baby book of a firstborn child is stuffed full.

Firstborn children tend to be perfectionistic, reliable, conscientious; they make lists, they are organized, critical, serious, and usually do well in school. If you can imagine the pressure heaped upon firstborns as magnifying these tendencies, you can probably pick out the anxiety problems that could result— performance anxiety, test anxiety, separation anxiety, obsessions and compulsions, the whole laundry list addressed in this book.

The firstborn has many similarities to the only child since he is the primary focus of his parent's life. All of the attention heaped upon a firstborn creates a tremendous amount of pressure to succeed, which can easily lead to a full-blown case of performance anxiety.

I have an oldest child who told me he hated being the eldest because his parents expected him to be "grown up." When he horsed around with his little brother, he got in double trouble because he was expected to set an example for his younger sibling.

Often parents forget that the firstborn *is* a child. Like all children, as they grow up, they will occasionally slip back. So when they are jumping on the bed with the youngest, they shouldn't get punished the most. Growing up is like a yo-yo— you act mature then immature, then mature then immature.

The Middle Child

The middle child is the mediator, has the thinnest baby book, and the fewest pictures in the photo album. She avoids conflict, is independent, is extremely loyal, has many friends, and forges her own way in the world.

The most difficult challenge for the parents of a middle child is to make her place in the family special. The middle child does tend to get ignored. She wears the hand-me-downs. She deals with growing up in the shadow of the shining star, the older brother or sister, which can lead to anxiety problems related to comparisons to the older child. Middle children tend to react with depression or temper. When they have temper outbursts, they are just making noise to stand out in the crowd. Take notice and the temper is likely to fade away.

As a solution, work hard to find that special something your middle child can be revered for, whether she says the best blessing at dinner or is the best kitchen helper. Find something she does that no one else in the family can do to help her find her place.

The Last-Born Child

This child, the baby of the family, is a master manipulator, quite charming, and a show-off. As a child and an adult, he blames others for his own mistakes and probably gets away with it. He loves people, and they love him. An engaging flirt, the youngest is a good salesman. He enjoys the stage and doesn't want to leave it.

Parents need to be careful not to smother their last born. Though he is the "baby" of the family, he needs to grow up and become independent, too. If you don't let him do that, you risk creating a case of separation anxiety that may take years to undo. Last-born children have a tendency not to try very hard—mainly because they don't usually have to. They are cushioned out of jobs that fall to their older siblings. The best thing you can do to counteract this is to focus on their exerting effort beginning in kindergarten and all the way up to college.

HOW TO DEAL WITH TYPICAL
SIBLING RIVALRIES

When parents at the end of their rope come to me with problems between siblings, the first bit of comfort I can offer them is that their situations are usually not unique. I hear the same problems from parents year in and year out. The greatest step parents can take to create peace in the family is to make sure that all rules pertain to everybody and are not age-appropriate. The punishments need to be exactly the same for everybody. The only differences should be shortened time periods for the younger children. Younger children have a shorter attention span, so time out, grounding, or curtailment of certain activities such as watching television should be shorter for younger kids. Parents need to realize that discipline should not be their primary focus. For a smoothrunning household they need to spend more time developing a rewards system than a punishment system.

Following are some common sibling rivalries and some general solutions I offer to parents.

Problem: Both of my children want to sit in the front seat of the car all of the time. How do I resolve their constant bickering each time we go for a ride?

This is probably one of the very first conflicts your children will have, and it will begin as early as age three. The simplest option is to take turns. Just like Baskin Robbins, have everybody take a number. You can switch daily or weekly, but I'd avoid switching on each ride in the car—soon they'll be wanting you to pull over during a trip for them to switch seats.

Problem: *My younger child wants to have the same freedoms as my older child and constantly is wanting to play with his toys.*

Each child needs to have something that is special to him. It may be a toy or a CD, but it's very special and is something that shouldn't be shared. It's a possession. So each child should be able to take out what is special to him and put it on a "my" shelf. Beyond that, you can negotiate sharing the other toys.

Some activities that involve safety have to have an age put on them. This is an absolute. Lay down the law and don't waiver: "You can't ride your bike into the street until you are seven... You can't get your ears pierced until you are eleven...." Don't say, "Your brother couldn't do this until...." Just state it as an absolute. This is a rule.

This situation can be very anxiety-producing for the younger child. Even though you work hard not to compare your children, they will compare themselves. It's a frustrating reality to your younger child that she is not as developmentally capable as her older brother or sister. She gets very tired of hearing "You are too young."

To keep all siblings happy, rely on the concept of sharing. Get very basic and tell her that she is sharing with her brother by letting him have time with his friends and his toys and his activities. "You are going to share with your brother by letting him play this game. Later, your brother is going to share with you and you'll get to have a friend over or we're going to go someplace that you like to go."

Don't encourage your older child to help your younger child with studies. In your child's eyes, this is pointing out weaknesses. One of the first things you hear from young children is "Me do it" when you try to help them with something. You wish they would say, "I don't know," but what you hear is, "I know, I know." It's better to get an outside tutor and not a family member.

Problem: My oldest child has always been so compliant, but my younger child is really difficult and challenging and is always picking fights. Now, my older child has started to challenge me, too.

Humans have a tendency to except and accept good, compliant, cooperative behavior. A lot of times, since we expect it, we fail to reward it. Your older child may have started to give you back talk because you haven't acknowledged his goodness. You have appreciated it, but you haven't let him know.

The older child in this situation will often experience anxiety and will act out because you've locked him into this "good boy" role. You haven't let him try on different attitudes; instead, you've let him know that you expect him to stay compliant because your younger child is so difficult. At the same time, this situation creates anger in your younger child because it looks as though you are "always picking on me and never picking on him."

This is a difficult situation because you're dealing with two very different temperaments. The best preventive medicine, though, is to learn how to appreciate each child as an individual. Start early by telling your children you appreciate their humor, or their ability to speak up, or their sweet disposition and good behavior.

Problem: My oldest son has moved away to college and I need his bedroom to give to a younger child. How do I make sure he still feels secure about his home here?

Many college kids go through depression or a lapse into anxiety when you take away their room, because this action can translate into "I'm not a member of the family anymore."

Suddenly, after years of having a place, they are a guest. Don't make a change like this without discussing it with your son or daughter. Tell them you are thinking about redoing the house and ask them for their advice. Point out that the two younger siblings need some growing room or that you need to make space for an office at home. Use logic and ask them to help find a solution. Then ask yourself what you can do to make the room special for your older child when he comes home for the holidays. Don't just erase this child's existence from the home when he goes off to college.

Problem: My older child has a stutter and some learning disabilities. My younger child doesn't have any of these problems and makes fun of the older one, especially when he attempts to talk at the dinner table.

You have to stop the younger child from making fun of his brother, and the sooner the better. Impress upon the younger one how important it is for him not to tease by not allowing him to be a part of the dinner group until he can abstain from this type of behavior. If your child is old enough to get an allowance, charge him a fee for every put-down you hear. If you don't want to involve money, the fee can be playtime or time on the computer or time watching television—some form of payment that involves an activity your younger child enjoys.

Then, at the dinner table, make sure you focus on listening to the older child. Try to avoid talking for him. Be tolerant and patient.

Problem: My child tells outlandish stories. I'm afraid she's developing into a liar. Should I just laugh at these stories?

Just as every school-age child wants to make A's for her parents, younger children tend to measure their worth by contributing information to you. They are usually very proud of what they're going to say, so when they're laughed or jeered at or teased, it can be devastating. You can inhibit children from talking at all by following what they say with, "No, that's not right," and then correcting their story. The best response parents can make is to compliment the child for telling a great story, for thier cleverness. Then change the subject. You've let them know you know the story isn't the truth, but it still has value as a "story."

PART III

The Tough Stuff

8

Anxiety and the Special Needs Child

BUILDING SECURITY WITH FREEDOM

For most parents, having a child with special needs is a shock. It's not what you plan for when you have your first baby shower. For nine months, you've fantasized about the perfect baby, the one who would grow up to fulfill all of your hopes and dreams. When that doesn't happen, when you have a child that is not "normal," all of your expectations have to be revamped.

It's hard to get rid of your fantasies, which is why so many parents can be taken advantage of by so-called miracle cures. When I first started teaching retarded children in the '60s, there was such a program that claimed it could make retarded children have normal I.Q.s. The program was based on the premise that these retarded children did not learn to creep and crawl correctly during their development. Part of the program involved having the parents get on the floor and creep and crawl with their children, the result supposedly being normal intelligence. Another theory blamed retardation on a lack of carbon dioxide, and so kids were made to breathe into a paper bag. These theories sound ridiculous and farfetched, but when I first started teach-

117

ing, I was overwhelmed by the number of parents who would put their hope into these programs only to be devastated when they didn't work.

Recently I had a flashback to those days when I heard about someone who purported that reading disabilities were due to motion sickness and middle ear disorders. Parents following this advice were giving their kids over-the-counter motion sickness medication. While indeed some children might respond to this treatment, it is not a panacea for all children with learning disabilities. By definition, children with learning disabilities or differences learn through untraditional approaches. So, a pill can't replace the material they will naturally miss in a traditional classroom situation.

It's hard for parents to give up their hopes, but for the sake of their special needs children, they need to embrace acceptance and realign expectations to fit their child.

Sometimes parents can't accept disabilities. My second day on the job as a staff psychologist at a children's hospital we had a phone call from a father who wanted the hospital to come and get his infant. The baby had been born two days earlier without lower arms and lower legs. The family was unable to accept the infant's disabilities because their life was so centered on sports. I worked and worked with this family, but none of them could reach a point of acceptance. Finally, in the child's best interest, we found a loving foster family.

Another patient who had rheumatoid arthritis was finally put into foster care because her mother, a single parent, was not able to fulfill her daughter's medical requirements. She had to be on a special diet and have medication several times a day, which overwhelmed her mother.

More often than not, though, I find that with help and support, families meet the challenge of their special children and receive much pleasure and satisfaction raising them. Following are some common hurdles that parents must overcome to get to that point.

WORK THROUGH THE GUILT

Many disabilities and illnesses are genetic, which means parents have to deal with the fact that they passed on these problems to their children. It's not easy, especially with diseases like cystic fibrosis (CF) or muscular dystrophy (MD), where the children have a shortened life-span.

Parents who can't deal with their guilt are often the ones who "doctor shop" until they find someone who gives them some hope for change. Others will pour themselves into foundation work, raising money for research, spending hour upon hour working for the cause. The downside of doing this is that they sacrifice the rest of their family. The parents may say they are doing this needed work for their child, but more often, they are only overcompensating out of guilt.

Not only can this extreme involvement in the cause damage the rest of the family, it can also harm the child who is suffering from the illness. When the parents involve the child in the cause, it takes away the child's ability to decide his own role in life. The child no longer has a choice because the parents are making him participate in order to satisfy their own drive to be MD or CF parent of the year. Just as with children with no disabilities parents need to consider their child's temperament. Will he enjoy the limelight? Or is he naturally shy? If he is shy, forcing him into poster-child status can be very anxiety-producing.

Parents can learn to deal with their guilt and how to cope with their special needs child by participating in parental groups offered by nonprofit agencies associated with their child's disease or disability. These groups will help parents work through the trials and tribulations, everyday demands, and the guilt. Parents in these groups share helpful hints for raising their children, and many of these ideas help doctors and technicians develop new techniques or appliances to be used with special kids.

Most pediatricians or physicians will also recommend that parents of special needs children go through genetic counseling. This process not only helps parents understand how the disability happened but will help them understand the odds of it happening again with another child.

Sometimes, though, disabilities just happen. Every pregnancy has a small risk for birth anomalies that do not have a determinable cause. The development of a child is so complex that you may never know what could have caused a problem. The risk of having genetic problems in a baby does increase with the age of the mother. There is a 1 in 450 chance for chromosome problems at age thirty, for instance; a 1 in 200 chance at age thirty-five, and a 1 in 65 chance for some problem at age forty. By age forty-five, the odds are 1 in 20.[1]

Down syndrome, caused by an extra chromosome, is the most common chromosomal abnormality. An extra chromosome can also cause heart defects and mental retardation. Genetic testing during pregnancy can be used to screen for these problems as well as for sickle cell disease, most prevalent among blacks; for Tay-Sachs disease, most common among Jewish people of eastern European descent; and for cystic fibrosis, most frequently found in people of northern European descent.

REALIGN EXPECTATIONS

Most kids, until they reach the age of about twelve, want to please their parents. When parents' expectations are beyond what children can achieve—as is often true in special needs cases— kids will keep trying even if they begin to suffer extreme anxiety.

With special kids, parents need to break down each task to small, attainable goals. Making the bed, for instance, can be overwhelming to a child with severe physical handicaps. But since the rest of the kids in the family are expected to make their beds, chances are the special needs child will want to try. The first step may be just pulling up the sheet. When that has been mastered and the child has experienced some success, move on to pulling up the blanket or the spread. That may be as far as some can go; with others, add putting the pillows on the bed. The key is to break every task down into small steps and to make sure your child is successful before you encourage him to move on to the next step. If he can't do it, go back a step and wait patiently. Let your child's frustration level be your clue to know when to stop pushing him. Remember, special kids often have developmental delays and sometimes you have to wait on maturity.

Try to rethink jobs that your normal kids do and tailor them to your special needs child. A child with cerebral palsy may not be able to handle taking out the kitchen trash. But buy a smaller trash can and make it a daily instead of weekly or every-other-day chore, and he may be able to master it. If not, step in and share the job, letting your special needs child help so he feels that he's part of the family with his own responsibilities.

HELP BUILD PEER RELATIONSHIPS

It's hard to get parents to accept their child's special needs, but it's even harder sometimes to get a child to accept those challenges and limitations. Helping that child build the strong peer relationships that can lead to that acceptance is one of the most difficult jobs a special child's parent has.

In spite of everything we do in society to remove the handicapped label, it's very difficult for a handicapped child to maintain a close friendship with an able child. The special child will want normal friends and may even resist a parent's efforts to encourage friendships with other handicapped children, but it's essential for your child to maintain both types of friendships. It is character building for non-handicapped children to have disabled friends.

Avoid getting get caught up in creating a "fake" world for your child by trying to keep her only in the mainstream. Relationships with normal kids are great, but if that's all your child has, you risk setting her up for frustration and depression when she realizes she has limitations her normal friends don't have. This is a competitive world, and the severely handicapped child cannot compete with the able-bodied child. The handicapped child can be easily frustrated playing with normal friends because she wants to win and the odds are not fair. The kids with whom they can be successfully competitive, though, are peers. It's among peers that your child will find lasting, lifelong friendships.

Sometimes it can be pretty lonely for a handicapped child. Those who are adept with a computer now have a whole new world available to them through the information highway. They may never see their computer friends, but they can have fulfilling friendships over the modem.

Another fertile place for friendships is in special programs like Special Olympics and therapeutic horseback riding. These types of programs set children up for success and help them make friends while giving parents a needed respite from what can be constant care. There are also various summer camps available for special kids that can cater to their special needs.

SUPPORT INDEPENDENCE

It's easy for parents of special children to be overprotective, to try to save them from hurt and failure in our competitive world. Parents of special needs children must find the happy medium between protecting and fostering their child's independence. You have to let your child try out new experiences and situations. Don't anticipate problems before they happen, or you'll end up restricting freedom and setting up your child for anxiety when he does venture out.

Parents of special children are afraid their child will be teased. So often, to protect their feelings, they will keep their child from going to new places and doing new things. In this respect, handicapped kids are only handicapped by normal adults. The reality is, a handicapped child probably will be teased, but the average cute, able child will also be teased for something. Again, let your child be the barometer. It may hurt you to watch your child fall in his leg braces or stumble due to lack of coordination, but if your child wants to try a sport, let him try.

Expose your special needs child to a wide range of experiences and he will find enjoyment and success. Mentally handicapped children do sometimes have what is called "splinter skills." Like the Rain Man, they may be great at math. They may not be able to read but will have a talent at the piano. I once had a patient who had been born prematurely. She was a slow learner and had vision problems that were blamed on her being incubated as an infant. Still, she found a vocation in crafting pottery. She was extremely talented.

NURTURE THE WHOLE FAMILY

Another challenge for the parents of a special needs child is to remember to care for the whole family. A special needs child does demand more attention, but parents have to find a balance. Involve your special needs child in supporting other family members in their efforts just as you involve the rest of the family in celebrating the successes of your special needs child.

I once helped a little boy who came from a large family with several siblings with muscular dystrophy. His parents had become so involved with his siblings that he felt neglected and resentful—and guilty for being the normal one. He began attracting attention by skipping classes and failing tests. Once his parents began to see him as clearly as they did their handicapped children, he began to feel better about himself.

There's a high incidence of divorce in these families because many times one of the parents cannot accept their part in making this handicapped child. I've known many fathers who have trouble accepting their child's disabilities. Deep down, they feel that it somehow reflects on their prowess.

Just as with all couples, parents of special needs children need to take time out for their own relationship. A healthy marriage is good for the whole family.

ENLIST THE TEACHER'S HELP

Whether your special child's problem is diabetes, severe asthma, hemophilia, limb deformities, cystic fibrosis, or learning disabilities, ask his teacher to take some time to give a lesson on the disease or disability to the class. Beginning in the first grade, kids have health class each year. The teacher may be able to ask the school nurse to come in and talk about various problems.

Kids notice differences and they'll have questions. Those with diabetes can't eat the same things as normal kids, those with asthma can't run hard at recess. Children will be less likely to tease and more likely to be understanding if they have some knowledge of the problem. If your child is not shy, talk to the teacher about centering a "show and tell" session around your child's handicap. If he has asthma, he can show classmates how his inhaler works. If he has an artificial limb, he can show how he uses it. With classmate curiosity eased, your child has a better chance of blending in to the playground scene.

I once had a patient who was born without her lower right arm. She was able to lead a lesson and show her artificial arm and hand and demonstrate how it worked. It helped her a lot to be able to answer questions and talk about her difference with the other kids. She took off her hand and passed it around the class. Afterward, she wasn't embarrassed about it any more.

TACKLING TREATMENT

Children who have special needs often must endure procedures and treatment that can be a source of extreme anxiety. One of my patients is a three-year-old with idiopathic scoliosis, which can be very progressive when it occurs in a young child. The treatment involves anesthetizing her and wrapping her in a tight body vest. The cast uses her hips and underarms as levers to essentially keep the spine straight. This child began life as an independent little girl, but being restricted physically and going through the traumatic experience of this treatment, essentially caused a post-traumatic stress disorder. She developed a severe stutter and began to regress developmentally.

In addition to sending this child to a speech therapist, she comes to my office where I try to give her a positive experience in a "medical" setting. She knows I am a "doctor," but my office is a fun place where she plays games, talks, and gets candy when she leaves. These nonthreatening visits work to counteract the trauma she's experienced in other medical situations. As she becomes more comfortable with these doctor visits, the body-casting treatments should become less traumatic.

With older children I try to get them to learn to separate their bodies from themselves to relieve anxiety. I help them to visualize their treatment or medicine as something their body needs and that can't hurt their real self. This type of thinking is also helpful in getting children to accept their handicaps without hurting their self-esteem. This may sound like I'm teaching kids to have split personalities, but I want them to identify physical not emotional limitations.

THE SPECIAL CHALLENGES OF IMMOBILITY

Kids with crutches, artificial legs, or severe lack of coordination often have a fear of falling. Going to football games, the circus, even a crowded hall at school can send them into a panic. Watch for signs of fear before you put your child into these mainstream situations. Physically handicapped kids who have normal mental functions will tend to push themselves too hard even when they're anxious. They sense that their parents wish they weren't handicapped, so they try hard to meet expectations—sometimes at the expense of a broken bone. Help your handicapped child test the water in these situations. Go to the football game early to get a good seat and avoid crowds. Stay late until the crowd has thinned. Your child will be more comfortable and you won't have to fight traffic, either. Give your child an out if he doesn't want to go to an event. At school, talk to the teacher about your child's fears. He or she may enlist your child's help with a task that allows him to leave early or come late to avoid the hall rush.

HOW TO DEAL WITH FATAL DISEASES

It's true that we all have to deal with death, but children with fatal diseases stare it in the face. This reality comes with its own set of anxiety problems. I once worked with a little girl who had a neuromuscular problem similar to MD. When she became a pre-teen, she started losing her friends with MD to the disease. She had grown up with them, and most of them weren't making it past the age of fourteen or fifteen. She became so fearful of dying that she would hyperventilate and have panic attacks. Eventually these got so severe that she had to be put on a ventilator. Even though she should have been able to breathe on her own, each time her doctors wanted to try taking her off the ventilator she would panic. I worked with her on various ways to try to relax and eventually got her to visualize herself off the ventilator. When she could do that without panicking, she was truly able to stay off the ventilator.

In these cases, I work with both the children and the families to help them discern between real and unreal fears. There are many ways to help a family come to grips with death. Some families rely on religion, others on research about near-death experience. Some families find their own unique comforts. I once had a patient with MD who found his own way to make peace with death. Each time one of his friends would die, he would have his mom take him to a hospital to see the babies. He felt like the babies were a replacement. They helped him view death as simply the final stage of the life cycle.

In these families especially, parents need to talk about death as a natural part of life from the time their child is a young age. Start with *Charlotte's Web* and progress to the more abstract explanations of death. The most important thing is to talk about it. Don't let death become a dark secret, a bogeyman in the closet.

THE RETARDED CHILD

The smarter you are, the more you'll suffer from anxiety problems. For this reason, most retarded children will be happy and carefree as long as they aren't pushed beyond their abilities. When I first began teaching retarded children, I noticed a relationship between problems with bed-wetting and thumb-sucking and high parental expectations. When parents were extremely intent on getting their children to read or count beyond their child's developmental level, we would have an outbreak of bed-wetting and thumb-sucking.

Once I got each child working at his own developmental level without being under a lot of stress or pressure, the bed-wetting and thumb-sucking would stop. If the pressure was turned up by parents, the problems returned.

Back in the early '60s, schools didn't integrate retarded and mainstream children. My retarded classes had to eat at a time when no other classes were in the cafeteria. Our recess was at a different time. We didn't go to assembly. But even with these limitations, I was determined to give my students a variety of experiences. I drove the school bus downtown to take them to see Santa Claus. Whatever came to town, I managed free tickets for the class. The kids were thrilled. They successfully handled pointing, laughing, and teasing because I taught them to respond with humor. I got them to laugh at themselves and get used to being called a "retard." I'd ask them, "Are you 'a retard?'" Initially they would respond with a defensive "No." But when I turned the taunts of other children into a joke in an attempt to insulate them, they began to accept their limitations, and at the same time the sting was removed from the taunts.

Many times parents feel worse than their children when their children are teased. Instead of teaching their child to laugh it off, and to accept good traits, they spend time soothing hurt feelings. This approach may help the parent but does nothing for the child. Instead, get retarded kids to laugh when they're clumsy. Kids who can laugh at their limitations accept them and get on with their lives.

THE GIFTED CHILD

Gifted children are often the children who know too much, and knowing too much can be anxiety-producing in and of itself. These children also have special needs and come with a set of problems uniquely their own.

One of the best ways to ward off anxiety is to help your gifted child find good friends. Because of their ability to think on a higher level, they have problems developing friendships. It's hard for them to find kids on the same plain as they are. With the popularity and complexity of computer games, gifted kids have a tendency to become overinvolved with computers and become reclusive. Parents need to seek out other gifted kids who their child will enjoy.

Boredom is another innate problem with gifted children. Many schools now have mentor programs where advanced kids can participate in learning about certain occupations in science, math, and other fields that tend to attract the gifted child. These programs can help keep gifted children active socially, and also act as a carrot to get them through what they consider the mundane or boring everyday schoolwork.

Gifted kids have a high risk of suffering from anxiety and fear of failure when they finally get to a level that challenges them. Because academics have come so easily to them, when they fail for the first time, it can be devastating. For this reason, it's important to give your gifted child the experience of having to accomplish a task that takes effort and tenacity. Succeeding is important, but succeeding after great effort is especially gratifying. A sport like golf is a good way to build humility. Being with peers in a mentor program also helps teach them that there are going to be challenges ahead in life. If they're exposed to smaller challenges from a young age, then they are less likely to be anxious when they experience difficult challenges for the first time.

THE CHILD WITH LEARNING
DISABILITIES

There are almost as many types of learning differences as there are numbers of children—kids with attention-deficit hyperactivity disorder (ADHD); those with learning disabilities involving fine motor coordination that affect handwriting skills; others with disabilities that make math difficult; auditory learners who have difficulty with written assignments; dyslexic children who struggle with vocabulary and the written word; and children who have problems in the spatial area or trouble with organization. These problems are real and many of them demand medication, special education, and special parenting techniques before the child will be successful. I expect that in the next ten years, education will become increasingly more specialized to handle such learning differences. But given today's educational limitations, you can't expect every teacher to cope with the special needs of your child and adapt the classroom style to help him.

As with any special need, it's important for parents to help their children accept that they have a learning difference and to understand it does not mean they aren't intelligent. Beginning in the first grade, children automatically associate being able to read with intelligence. If they have any difficulty learning to read, they will become anxious and fearful that they are dumb. Learning disabilities are "unseen" disabilities and are difficult to explain to children.

Kids are individuals, and have different learning styles. But in a classroom situation, where kids compare themselves to one another, those with learning differences feel more pressure, and pressure makes their struggles even harder.

Parents need to keep in mind that kids with learning disabilities are constantly comparing themselves not only to other kids in their classroom but also to their own siblings. If an older brother gets A's and another child has learning differences and grinds out C's and D's, be extra careful about handing out strokes for grades. Remember to reward the effort as well as the result. Find something your learning disabled child excels at that gives him his own special status in the family.

Many parents get caught up in making their learning disabled child feel "normal," when in reality, he isn't. Keeping learning disabled children in a mainstream, so-called normal school may be the worst thing for some of them. If they are in a special school with other kids whose learning styles are similar, they may be far less anxious. When they succeed, their self-esteem will soar.

Another solution for some kids is to hold them back a year in school. I don't recommend doing this any later than kindergarten because your child will never forget that her friends moved on ahead of her and will have a hard time not believing it wasn't because she was dumb. Happily, I'm finding more and more schools that have a preprimary transitional grade between kindergarten and first grade. This is a great solution for the child who needs a little more time developmentally. The kids are still academically challenged, and they have more time to mature before moving on to the first grade.

Parents of learning disabled kids need to be especially careful of not projecting their own wants, goals, and expectations onto their children. If you signed your child up for the "right" preschool before birth only to find out that preschool does nothing to help your child developmentally, you may be setting your child up for anxious times ahead. The "right" school is the one that will understand your child's special needs, not necessarily the one that feeds into the "right" elementary school and the "right" prep school and the "right" college.

Don't set up your learning disabled child for failure by expecting him to keep up with the Joneses. In one such situation, a family kept their learning disabled son in an elite school by being benevolent when the annual fund drive came around. The school was small and catered to honors-type students. Out of a class of thirteen, more than half of the class consistently had perfect averages. So even when this boy made C's, which was excellent for him, he was at the very bottom of his class. Not surprisingly, after competing with those kids for so long, he felt he was stupid and doomed to fail. He is so anxious now about failing that his anxiety has become a self-fulfilling prophecy. He has taken college history twelve times and never completed the course.

I encourage parents who suspect their child has learning problems to get a thorough evaluation early on—at the preschool level—so they can begin making plans about the best way to educate their child. Then, as with other special needs children, I help them prepare their child for success instead of failure by setting reasonable goals. With each successful move, no matter how small, you create more confidence that will eventually suppress and perhaps eliminate the anxiety.

If these children do become anxious—and they are at special risk for test anxiety—biofeedback can be very useful in helping them learn to handle and deal with anxiety as it comes up. I use a device called the Galvanic Skin Response (GSR), which is available at Radio Shack and other electronics stores. It has been around for sixty-five years and monitors the electrical resistance of the skin with a meter and an audible tone to gauge nervous-system activity. High stress or anxiety is indicated by a high-pitched tone. Kids can learn to relax by working on diminishing the tone or dial of the GSR to the lowest point. It becomes a game to them, and they soon learn to use deep breathing and visualization to make the tone and meter fall. When they master these skills with the GSR, they can use them anywhere, in any situation whenever they become anxious. The GSR teaches them that they can control their anxious feelings just as they control the tone or the arrow on the meter.

With some learning disabilities, most notably ADHD, medication has a proven success record. For many ADHD kids Ritalin is a miracle drug. One of my ADHD patients once stormed into my office claiming to have had a horrible day. He had been doing well for some time, and I was surprised. But as he poured out his troubles (he had gotten in trouble every step of the way) I began to suspect he hadn't taken his medication, which proved to be correct. Most often ADHD kids do not sense the difference medication makes in their lives, so they don't think they need it. It's important to reinforce with them that the medication is something their body needs—not something they need. The Ritalin helps everything run smoothly in their heads so they don't get to the point of extreme frustration.

Kids don't grow out of learning differences, but they do learn to deal with them. Specialized tutoring can raise their capabilities up to a level that will let them be successful in a regular school class. Most public schools are willing to aid a student by modifying assignments or allowing oral evaluations.

Your child may not be able to change her learning difference, and you may not be able to remove anxiety-producing situations from her life. But with the right guidance, she can learn to control the way she reacts to those situations, which is a tool that will help her throughout life.

9

Phobias, Panic, and Obsessive-Compulsive Disorders

A NEED FOR ORDER
IN CHAOTIC LIVES

It's normal for children to have some concerns about their lives. The younger they are, the more these concerns center around doing well in school. When these concerns escalate into worries, children can have symptoms of the various forms of anxiety that have already been discussed. If those anxieties escalate further, though, and begin to travel around and around in a child's brain without ever reaching a point of solution, preventing the child from being able to focus on school or enjoy life, then it's time to get some help.

When your child is worrying about things outside of the norm of his world—worrying about the end of the world, for example, or about whether Korea is going to unleash a nuclear bomb on the United States—chances are anxieties have become phobias. When these bizarre worries keep your child from his normal activities or provoke a panic attack, parents need to take immediate action.

If you have begun to notice any unusual habits in your child—habits that are outside of your normal realm of experience—your child could be developing obsessive-compulsive disorder. Children with these problems usually have an underlying need for order. The feeling of anxiety is a feeling of helplessness, and somehow a compulsion or obsession eases phobic fears and gives the child a sense of control. If I have a social phobia, for instance, and am terrified of being criticized or made fun of at an upcoming party, then I may sit in a room for hours combing my hair and getting ready. If I comb my hair long enough, I may miss the function altogether. In this example, not only does the compulsion ease the fear, it also helps the child avoid the fear. Parents shouldn't let these habits go on for too long before they consult a professional, because in my experience, obsessive-compulsive habits are hard to break.

One approach that has recently begun to show more and more success with obsessive-compulsive disorders is cognitive behavior therapy. With this therapy, psychologists work to identify the situations in which the obsessions or compulsions occur and then work through the child's thought processes, changing them to stop the behaviors. As you read through the following descriptions of these various disorders, you may notice similarities to behaviors in your own child. If you do, you should contact a nearby university or medical school and ask them to recommend psychologists or doctors who are trained to work with these phobias and may be proficient in cognitive behavior therapy.

PHOBIAS AND PANIC DISORDERS

A phobia is an anxiety disorder that involves a morbid and irrational fear of a specific object or situation. Often, even the child will realize that the fear is unreasonable or unwarranted; still, he must avoid the feared object to prevent panic.

In one such case, the patient had a fear of going through a doorway with other kids at school. She would skip lunch, or delay it, to keep from having to go through doors while other people were around. She also had other obsessive-compulsive tendencies. If she was doing math, she had to have ten problems in a row, and if there wasn't room on the page, or if there were more than ten problems, she would panic.

With phobias, it's hard for parents to understand that they can't just tell their kids, "It's silly to think that." The thoughts do seem silly or completely irrational—that's the nature of the disorder. It is more effective, though, for a doctor or psychologist to talk about these difficulties with the child in a logical way. Children automatically believe their parents aren't objective and don't understand, and someone outside of the family will have far more power to help your children work through these illogical thoughts that plague them. Be understanding. Your child does not enjoy his fears any more than you do.

OVERANXIOUS DISORDER

General anxiety can become so severe that a patient is diagnosed with overanxious disorder. This disorder is characterized by excessive worry and symptoms including restlessness, being easily fatigued, having your mind go blank, general irritability, muscle tension, and sleep disturbance. With these patients, worry is almost constant and keeps them from accomplishing tasks in school or chores at home. These kids seem distracted and are very easily frustrated. Even small frustrations can send them into a panic.

In addition to other approaches, I find that Nintendo and Sega are great tools for teaching these children how to handle frustration. You cannot be successful at any of these computer games unless you're able to curb your sense of frustration or panic. At the first sign of frustration, I get children to punch the pause button, get up, and regroup. Stopping the game helps them train themselves to rethink a situation when they become frustrated and before they panic. When they're calm and have a new plan of attack, then they start the game again.

I had one patient, a ten-year-old, who would become so absorbed in her thoughts and worries that she was afraid to leave home or go to sleep at night. In our sessions, we would talk about her worries; usually, there was a little bit of reality in them. I would use logic with her and talk about the percentages and probabilities of these things happening to her. It's impossible to tell a small child that something will never happen to her parents, but when you're dealing with a child, often you can talk about the fact that nothing has happened to her parents in the ten years this child has been alive and that chances are, everything will continue to be okay. Working through each worry in simple, logical steps, and reinforcing these steps week after week, can help ease anxiety.

NAUSEA PHOBIA

Another patient of mine had a phobia about becoming nauseated. His mother had moved out of the house when he was eight years old, leaving him and his two sisters with their father. The night his mother left, he came down with a stomach virus and vomited uncontrollably. Most kids want their mother when they're sick, but his mother was gone. From that point on, he had an irrational fear of throwing up. He would panic around anyone who got sick. I didn't see him until he was in high school, six years after the onset of his phobia. By that time, his mother had gotten her feet on the ground financially and the children were again living with her.

Since nausea phobia usually begins immediately after an illness or hospitalization that involved nausea, it didn't take us long to determine the root cause of this case. We immediately began to work through his feelings about his parents' separation and ultimate divorce. When he began to understand why he had developed the phobia, it helped reduce episodes of panic. At the same time, his pediatrician prescribed medication for anxiety that eased symptoms. Finally, when we reduced his anxiety about relationships, which he was experiencing because of his parents' separation, the phobia began to disappear.

Nausea phobia is not related to eating disorders like anorexia or bulimia, although these disorders should certainly be screened when children have an unnatural fear of vomiting. With true nausea phobia, a successful approach has involved instructing parents to ignore the child's symptomatic behaviors while at the same time supporting new behaviors with strict rules, especially at mealtime. Rules include no special meals, no snacks between meals, no dessert, and forfeiting other privileges if meals are left unfinished, no conversations about food, and praising the child when he finishes his meal.

FEAR OF SUICIDE

I once treated a little boy who was afraid he was going to commit suicide. He was not depressed, and was doing well in his fifth-grade class. He didn't know anyone who had committed suicide. There were no family problems that should have made him feel insecure. No one close to him had died—not even a pet. Yet he had this recurring thought that he was going to kill himself one day, and he didn't want to do it. He began to refuse overnights with friends because he was afraid his thoughts would take control of him and his fear would come true. He would panic, burst into tears, and fall completely apart whenever his parents left the house.

Since the root of his problem was unclear, we began to talk about the reality of suicide—that it was something one did to oneself and if he didn't want to do it, then he wouldn't do it. We talked about his own will being strong enough to keep him from being afraid of his thoughts and strong enough to make his thoughts go away when he wanted them to go away. It took us about eight visits before he learned to be more comfortable with himself and less afraid.

SCHOOL PHOBIA

School phobia is a panic disorder that occurs primarily in children who have an underlying separation anxiety problem. Sometimes a school phobia will surface after a child has been ill and stayed home for a week or two. Staying home with mother for more than a few days can bring back separation problems that the child may have overcome years before.

It's imperative for parents to stand their ground in these cases, and in spite of the child's protests, to keep trying to get the child back in school. In my experience, if kids are allowed to stay home when they put up a fight, the problem only grows worse. As they fall further behind in school, the panic increases. Some kids with school phobia can work themselves into a panic and make themselves physically ill to prevent having to go back to classes. When school phobias get to the point of no return, the only alternative may be hospitalization. Being put in the hospital makes the child and the parents realize how serious the problem is and can sometimes help them to work harder toward a solution. Also, the hospital is a safe, controlled environment where a child cannot hurt himself. When the situation becomes this severe, separation anxiety isn't the only problem. Chances are, there are serious marital problems.

I had one eleven-year-old patient who would hide under her bed, lock herself in her room, or climb out the window to avoid going to school. Finally, this case got so bad that she threatened her parents with a knife if they insisted on her going to school. Once at school, she would run away as soon as her parents drove away. Her tactics became so extreme that we were afraid she was going to hurt herself or someone else. She was admitted to a hospital where we began intensive therapy and finally began to learn what was behind the school phobia. The child felt intense pressure from her father to perform, and after failing to meet his standards, she had given up on succeeding or even trying. Other children in the family had also had problems with the father. An older sibling had refused to talk to him for more than a year. The mother in the family had been in therapy herself to help her deal with his unrealistic expectations.

As we worked with the entire family, the father could tolerate only so much admission of fault. When it reached a point he could not accept, he walked out of the therapy sessions. Eventually, the couple divorced. Their daughter was in the hospital for two months before we saw enough progress to try school again. But I'm happy to report that she finally began to enjoy school and do well.

To work with school phobias, I teach children relaxation techniques and use their previous successes in school to convince them that they are intelligent and capable of success. We begin with a gradual reintroduction to her school routine—going for one period for three days—then begin a rapid increase of time spent at school. I help them learn to incorporate the relaxation techniques they learn in my office into their everyday life at school, whenever they feel as though they might panic.

I have found both private and public schools to be cooperative in cases of school phobia. The key is to get the child back into school as quickly as possible. Parents will often try to bribe the child back into returning with new clothes, new supplies, even a new teacher. This usually doesn't work. The problem is inside of the child, not on the outside. You have to start with the root of the phobia.

Less acute forms of school phobia can last a lifetime. I have one twenty-five-year-old patient who's trying to complete college. It is so difficult for him because he has constant panic attacks related to school. He's never been able to complete even one semester. He'll drive to school, but then sit in his car, incapable of getting out and walking through the doors into class.

This patient has a history of learning disabilities, complicated by having to cope with a very critical family that's obsessed with performance in school. Since his family is convinced he's not succeeding, he feels guilty, which only exacerbates the problem. He has the desire to succeed and the talents to make a good teacher. He has had considerable experience and success working with special children in an agency where he does not need a degree, but the family pressure to get a degree remains constant.

On two different occasions he has attempted to go away to college, but panic has prevented him from completing a term. We have worked on relaxation and biofeedback and have begun to tackle college in smaller increments. Thankfully, many colleges now offer classes in mini-semesters. We are going to try those one class at a time.

This patient had a very successful older brother who was Mr. Everything in high school. Meanwhile, this patient was put in a special school and was constantly nagged by a perfectionistic mother. He couldn't do anything right in her eyes because he was by nature disorganized. This pressure created in him an obsessive fear that he couldn't do anything right. As an adult, these fears have become a self-fulfilling prophecy that has prevented him from having success in school, in jobs, and in personal relationships.

The ultimate answer in this case is a combination of therapy and a supportive family.

AGORAPHOBIA

Agoraphobia is a fear of open spaces. Kids with this problem have difficulty going by themselves or with friends or family to stores or anywhere there's a lot of movement or activity. The hustle and bustle in the halls at school creates panic. The adrenaline flow begins, they hyperventilate, and then they freeze. With these patients, relaxation techniques are essential to helping them through their day. Once I get them to master these techniques in my office, we try them out in the real world. I talk to them about the concept of control. They can learn to control their own bodies and how their bodies react to various situations. We replay scenes that inspired a panic or anxiety attack and talk through them. When patients begin to get anxious, we stop and I let them get control.

We talk about how they can choose situations that are less stressful to them. Rather than shopping on crowded Saturdays, they can go early on Sundays when there is less activity in the stores. As soon as they begin to feel anxious, they can leave before the onset of an attack. If they continue to get out in this manner, they will eventually become desensitized to the situations that once inspired panic. Most often this process has to be complemented with medication.

FEAR OF DYING

When a child has a fear of dying, it often translates into an extreme fear of being separated from his mother. I had one such patient and on our first day I told him it was my job to help him to achieve such independence. His response was a chirpy and resistant, "Good luck." When I asked him if he wanted to be happier and more independent, he said, "No."

The treatment for this little boy was basically the same as for separation anxiety (see Chapter 5) except that being a severe case, it took seven months before we began to make progress.

OBSESSIVE-COMPULSIVE DISORDER

Obsessive-compulsive disorder (OCD) is an advanced stage of anxiety where certain repeated actions or behaviors help reduce an internal anxious feeling. The old term "worry wart" comes to mind here—constant worry is a common type of obsession.

Obsessions are recurrent, persistent thoughts, impulses, or images that intrude upon normal thoughts and cause a child to be distressed. They are not just excessive worries about real-life problems, but are about out-of-the-ordinary, improbable events. Serious obsessions are unwelcome thoughts that don't go away even if the child wants them to. Compulsions are repetitive behaviors or mental acts that children feel compelled to perform. These behaviors are aimed at preventing or reducing the stress associated with the obsession. If the child is kept from performing the act, the anxiety escalates.

When these obsessions and compulsions interfere with normal functioning, they have become a disorder.

Usually the strange habits of someone suffering from OCD are things they do in preparation for beginning a task. If they don't go through their rituals, they can't begin. This does not mean people suffering from OCD cannot be successful. I had a patient—an attorney—who took an hour and a half to select a pen. The habits of people suffering from OCD keep them from developing a flow to their performance. Often kids will be obsessively neat, have to have their books stacked a certain way, their bedspreads perfectly straight, everything in order before they can begin to do homework. These children are trying to bring some degree of order and control into their lives.

The anxieties and the fears themselves have a pattern to them. They'll begin thinking of one fear and move on to others in a set pattern. The behaviors serve to reduce the anxiety, and when the behaviors don't work, they panic. Often children suffering from OCD will have tics or physical habits like shaking their head, or touching the arm of a chair over and over, or tapping a foot or a pencil.

One little girl with OCD would walk down the halls of her school in a set pattern in order to control her anxious feelings. Another example of repeated behavior is the child who has to check the alarm and the locks on the doors and windows repeatedly before he can get ready for bed, even though the family has never experienced crime. Whatever these actions are, if they begin to interfere with normal activities, parents need to seek professional help. In the meantime, parents should avoid teasing the child or letting other members of the family make fun of the child's habits. This will only make the problem worse.

Kids who fear being teased about their appearance sometimes develop compulsions in their dressing habits. They may continue to comb their hair for hours, never getting it right. They may become obsessed with their weight. I have had little girls express fear of obesity as early as third grade. They may be anxious about their clothes being perfect. Nothing is clean enough or perfect enough.

Obsessive cleaning is a common type of OCD. I had one ten-year-old patient who couldn't stand for anyone to touch his clothes. He wanted all of his laundry done every day and became very agitated if it wasn't. He had been diagnosed with irritable bowel syndrome at the age of sixteen months, had suffered from projectile vomiting, and had always been an anxious, fearful child. He never could sleep in a room by himself, so his mother let him sleep in a twin bed in her room. He had always been intolerant of noise. As he grew up, he developed the OCD behavior in cleaning habits. His mother would come home to find him cleaning his room, the house, doing laundry. Everything had to be perfect or his coping mechanisms would break down.

The use of anxiety medication along with cognitive therapy can help reprogram thinking to help a child focus more on comforting thoughts and less on fears. "The probability of an atomic war is less now than it was for many years." "Your parents do come home from work every night." "Your father did come home safely from his last business trip."

With OCD, I often hear parents lament that their children are "just like me." More and more research indicates that OCD is an inherited trait since so many kids who have it have a family member who exhibits similar symptoms.

One case involved a little boy who had a wide variety of tics and compulsions. Though neither parent had tics, his grandmother did have some of the same symptoms. The following poem was written by that grandmother to her grandson, and gives you a glimpse into the mind of someone who suffers from a form of a tic disorder.

Tim's grandmother wrote this for him after her son, Tim's father, told her how much the boy's habits bothered him. Now Tim, who adores his grandmother, has it framed and hanging in his room.

BIRDS OF A FEATHER

Tim, I apologize for the legacy I may have left you
Not on purpose, I assure, but nevertheless true
Ever since I was your age I was accused
Of the manners and etiquette I totally abused.

Nanna asked, "What's wrong," and Anne said, "Don't
embarrass me"
Because I was constantly pulling on my panties, you see
And then I kept picking, picking, picking at my nose
What I was after, me nor no one else knows.

When Uncle Bob was here last he asked, "Why are you
coughing hacky?"
I had no answer—I couldn't help it—but knew it was tacky.
And John on his July visit asked, "Gramma, are you sniffing?"
I thought—but I already knew I had no answer uplifting.

Then there was a time I went through a spell
Of blinking and blinking my eyes as well
Oh I've done them all—the things that are strange
That makes me, as well as others, want me to change.

Tim, I just think we are a specialty of genes
Because no one else understands our obnoxious schemes.
Who can we blame it on and not say it's our own dilemma?
Who can we blame it on—maybe Nanna Johnson—or Emma?

Tim, I hate to have these habitual quirks
Because it makes the rest of the family smirk.
I've had them all of my life and probably always will
But in spite of what we do, I think they will love us still.

They're not perfect—just look at some of the things they do
Kelly talks weird—Steve burps and sticks his retainer out,
Mom and Dad "coo."
We will master our "habits" one of these days
And in the meantime, they must accept our ways.

If they don't—we'll just stick together
And say, "Birds of a Feather."

10

Anxiety and Divorce
KEEPING FAMILIES TOGETHER
WHEN PARENTS PART

There's no way around it—divorce is tough on every member of the family. But if parents put their children first, children can emerge from a divorce healthy and happy and without the lasting anxiety problems that can keep them from having good relationships in the future. You can be a good model and preserve a sense of family for your child even when your marriage is ending.

It's easy for parents, caught up in the turmoil of a divorce, to forget that their marital relationship is a model for their children's future relationships. If a child is exposed to parental arguments and parents' who fail to communicate, it will set him up for similar difficult relationships when he is an adult.

A divorce is one of the most stressful situations you can face in your life. But by stopping to consider your children at the various stages of your marital relationship—before, during, and after your divorce—you can minimize the negative effects of that stress on your children and hopefully prevent the anxiety problems that divorce can cause.

PREPARING YOUR CHILD FOR A DIVORCE

Whether you argue in front of your child or not, remember, she is very attuned to your body language and will know when something is wrong. It's best to sit down and talk to your child when you and your spouse are having difficulties. Tell your child that mom and dad are having some problems at the present time, but that she is not part of those problems.

When talking to young children, equate your fighting to something they can understand. "You know when you have an argument with Amanda, she's still your friend, but you may not like to be with each other for a couple of days. Well, your Dad and I are having a disagreement sort of like that."

Attempt to do your disagreeing out of the reach of your child's ears. Behind closed doors isn't good enough. Meet somewhere away from home during the day for your discussions. If you've decided there's no way marital counseling will work, consider using a mediator to help you resolve preliminary issues even before you begin final divorce proceedings.

When you've decided that divorce is inevitable, buy an age-appropriate book about divorce for your child and read it to him to help explain how his life is going to change. The younger the child, the more insecure he will be about a divorce. Divorce is a concept that is very difficult for young children to understand because parents seem to be feeding them two sets of information. "We love you, but we don't like each other," is a complicated concept for a small child. If Daddy is leaving the home, a small child's first fear will be that Mommy will leave, too. It's not uncommon during a divorce for a small child to regress and act like a baby, become clingy, and begin to exhibit signs of separation anxiety. If your child is behaving this way, you and your spouse need to spend more time with him talking about the divorce and assuring him that you both love him as much as you always did. Other things may change; your love for him will remain constant.

With older children, it's best to briefly explain that you and your spouse can't get along and then spend more time talking about what will really concern your child—what life is going to be like after the divorce. There are going to be a lot of changes, and it will give your child a feeling of some stability if he knows what to expect in the coming months. Be honest and don't sugarcoat if you're going to have a tough time financially. The most comforting thing you can do for your child right now is to let him know what's going to happen and exactly how it's going to affect him. Don't guess at changes. Wait for facts.

Teenagers can react to a divorce in a wide variety of ways, possibly with disgust, sometimes with pleasure. Parents are less likely to hide their arguments from an older child, so your teenager will know all too well that life around the house has been hell for too long. A teenager is in the process of trying on relationships for himself, so a prolonged predivorce stage can be more anxiety-producing for a teenager than for a small child. Teenagers are like little children in that they're very self-centered. "What's going to happen to me?" is their central worry. Is this going to blow college? Are we going to have to move to a different high school away from my friends?

Parents need to understand that children react to the divorce process itself, not the reasons for the divorce. Divorce creates change, so your child needs to know what's going to happen. He doesn't need to know it's happening because Dad or Mom had an affair. Be sure to separate your adult problems from the problems that your child will have to deal with. A kid is only interested in such questions as, Where am I going to live? Who am I going to live with? Can I go to the same school? Is Daddy ever coming back? Will he still love me?

Give your child as much detail as you can about your living situation when you know it. If you may have to sell the house, tell her that but let her know that you're trying to keep her life as stable as possible by finding a place to live where she won't have to change schools.

Don't answer for the other parent if your child has questions that should be asked of him or her. Encourage your child to have a conversation with your spouse to get those questions answered. When one parent is absentee, there is a tendency for the other parent to try to compensate. Don't fall into a trap of making excuses that will set up false expectations for your child. ("Your Dad is really busy these days, but I'm sure he'll make it to your next game.") You'll only make your child more frustrated, and you'll end up dealing with the force of that frustration.

It's much easier on your child if you are honest. Don't create a "fantasy Dad" when the real father will never fulfill those promises. Fantasies can create disappointments that are harder to deal with than the shortcomings of the real father.

Unlike a small child, an elementary school child doesn't need to be assured that the divorce is not their fault. They will have their own opinions about why the marriage failed. Where your child lays the blame can result in a loss of respect for one or both parents. During this time, there's a great possibility that your child will turn up the heat on testing and challenging your authority and rules.

HELPING YOUR CHILD COPE DURING A DIVORCE

No matter how hard you try, the odds are against your having an amicable divorce. In my experience, divorces may start out with good intentions on both sides, but the process of divorce itself is cruel and unusual punishment that will beat the civility out of even the most well-meaning couple. Marriages are filled with feelings and memories. Divorce court reduces feelings to material symbols, tries to put them on paper, and then tear them in half. It doesn't work. As the conflict between parents grows, the child becomes an object that is traded back and forth, and possession of that object becomes each parent's quest. Think about the language you use with one another. You talk about "trading weekends," "swapping holidays." In court, your child is a commodity.

In the worst of cases, the child is made to testify, usually in the judge's chambers. I have a difficult time with this and don't ever recommend it. It often pits the child against one or even both parents, and it's hard for the child to avoid feeling guilty when talking about his parents to a judge. This is an extremely anxious situation for a child, and I don't think it's a risk worth taking for either parent. The courtroom atmosphere is very intimidating to a child. A judge looks imposing in a big, black robe. Even the word "chambers" is strange. And from watching television, your child knows that judges usually deal with criminals.

The high cost of divorce isn't only emotional. If you can avoid a prolonged battle, there will be far more monetary resources left over for your children. You may be able to save the price of a college education if you can only stay out of divorce court. I highly recommend that all couples at least try mediation. For a couple of thousand dollars—less if you qualify for nonprofit services that charge fees on a sliding scale based upon income— you can work through your conflicts with a mediator, then have the judge finalize your agreement in a matter of minutes. The hours saved in legal fees are tremendous, and every dollar you save means there is more left for your children.

Sometimes, of course, it's necessary for judges to set boundaries for parents who are unable to understand what they're doing to their children. But more often, the divorce becomes a battle for attorneys who play the game of delay and postponement. Keeping the divorce situation in flux is terrible for children and makes them constantly anxious until it is resolved. For children, a year is an eternity since they go through so many developmental stages during that time.

During a prolonged and tumultuous divorce, your child is at risk to develop many anxiety problems. Perhaps the most common one is a fear of failing either parent, thus developing a case of performance anxiety. Children have a hard time knowing how to keep their loyalty to each parent intact without causing the other parent to become angry. One twelve-year-old patient once told me that he felt like he was being torn in half.

The younger the child, the more serious the risk for this problem because of a young child's tendency to believe he has caused the split. For a child under age five, the house has been child-oriented all of his life. Now, suddenly, Mom and Dad are preoccupied with their own problems, so the child naturally feels he's being punished. The final arguments of a dissolving relationship only reinforce these feelings since they usually center around expenses that have to do with the child—school tuition, soccer fees, child support. All a child has to hear is his own name somewhere in an argument, and he'll feel responsible.

Watch your child. Does she act like she's on pins and needles? Is she working too hard to please, to bring home the best grades? If so, she may be trying to cure the situation somewhere. That's your clue to have another conversation about divorce, explaining that it has nothing to do with her or anything she has done. In addition to becoming perfectionists, kids will sometimes take on a caretaker role following a divorce. This is especially true if one parent goes on with his life and the other one remains miserable about the divorce. Boys especially will try to be the big man around the house and will feel responsible when Mom is unhappy. Later, if Mom tries to introduce a new person into the household, this son has a really tough time adjusting to his loss in status.

Just as with any traumatic situation, it's a good idea to have periodic conversations with your child about the divorce throughout the years, since as he grows and matures, he will have a greater understanding of the situation and more questions for you.

As your child turns twelve, he may decide that he wants to live with his other parent—usually the same sex parent if he has lived with the opposite sex parent for a number of years. This can bring on anxiety problems since it's a difficult subject for the child to bring up, and he will try not to hurt the feelings of the parent he has been living with until now. Children at this age are still extremely vulnerable to being pressured or made to feel guilty by a parent. An unhappy parent can do great damage by laying on subtle guilt. I once had a patient whose nonmanaging parent made a habit of making "I miss you when you're not here" a part of daily conversation with the child. It's so easy to make a child feel responsible for taking care of an unhappy parent. You don't have to say, "I have no one here when you're gone"; a simple "I can't wait until you come back" gets that message across loud and clear.

If you make a habit of saying these things to your child, explore your motives. You may think you're letting your child know how important and valuable she is to you, but in effect you're putting guilt on your child that can easily create problems with anxiety. Your child is in a frustrating Catch 22 bind: She's fearful of getting too attached to the parent she is living with, and afraid that the parent she doesn't live with will think she's not loyal. This child will begin to put pressure on herself in every aspect of her life—school, sports, her behavior at home. When she isn't perfect, she'll fall apart. Kids like this develop general anxiety, as they begin to fear that every failure will threaten their relationship with their parents.

If one parent abandons the family, there is a tendency for the remaining parent to hover over the child to assure him that the parent wasn't abandoning him but abandoned the marriage. If either parent leaves it's traumatic for a child, but with small children, it's especially difficult for the child when the mother leaves. There is no other way for this child to interpret her leaving other than that she did not want to mother him. So everyone left steps in to reassure the child that it wasn't his fault. It's easy to overdose on this kind of compensatory attention. Your child will see through it and will then question whether what you say is true. The parent who left is not available to explain why he left, so the doubt and wonder will remain with the child until he can ask those questions of the missing parent. It will be difficult for your child to be comfortable with anyone else's explanation. Instead of trying to overcompensate, it's better for you to allow your child to go through a needed process of denial, loss, grief, anger, and acceptance. If your child can't go through these steps by himself, then he may need professional help.

GIVING YOUR CHILD A SENSE OF FAMILY
AFTER A DIVORCE

Restore Stability

After a divorce, one of the best things you can do is try to restore stability in your child's life. If you can, work with your ex-spouse to set up similar rules and routines in both houses, which will give your child a feeling of continuity and comfort. This is difficult when one parent has only weekend visitation, because kids don't have to get up for school on the weekends. But bedtime, mealtime, bath time, and study time should be standardized. Also, make sure your child has responsibilities at both households so that one parent isn't seen as easy and the other one as the heavy.

One ten-year-old patient who lived primarily with his father had trouble getting schoolwork done at his mother's house. Instead of telling his mother that he had to study, he would go along with whatever activities his mom had planned, afraid he would hurt her feelings. Then when he did poorly on tests, he'd get in trouble with his dad. This situation could have been prevented if there had been a set study time at Mom's house just as there was at Dad's.

Once you have established post-divorce living arrangements, don't bring up the question of change. Assume your child is happy with the present arrangement unless he tells you otherwise. He will hear about all kinds of custody arrangements from friends at school. During pre-teen years there is a natural curiosity for children to want to live with the same-sex parent. Often they are curious to see what it would be like to live with the other parent. When it's their decision, and when the other parent is cooperative, give it a trial run. He'll come back if it's not meant to be. Often a child who has lived with Mom for a number of years will think there will be more latitude at Dad's house. When Dad turns out to be just as strict as, or more than, Mom, that child may want to return to Mom's house.

During adolescence, children look for same-sex role models.

If it's impossible for children to get that influence from an ex, make an effort to find a feminine or masculine influence for them. A dad might start taking his daughter to the beauty shop, for instance, or find a dress store with a helpful saleswoman who will work with his daughter and help her select clothes. There are also classes given by department stores that teach makeup techniques, hair styling, and how to work with clothes styles. Children at this age are naturally anxious about their appearance and need a role model to help them know how to dress and how to act.

Don't Criticize Your Ex-Spouse

Divorced parents need to make every effort to be civil to one another. It's a confusing relationship for your children because they love you both, but you don't love one another. If you can at least like each other, it can ease their anxiety over this question.

On the other hand, getting along too well can fuel false hope for your kids that you'll get back together. For years after a divorce, kids will harbor fantasies of reconciliation. Make it clear to your children that a divorce is a separation and don't confuse them by doing all the things together as a family that you did before the divorce. Your child's family is essentially two separate but equal units—one at Dad's house, the other at Mom's.

That doesn't mean that parents shouldn't do some things together for the sake of their children. If your child is going to have to start a new school as a result of your divorce, take him to school together. You should also be able to both go to soccer games, recitals, and so on. Sit together if you can do it without arguing so that your child doesn't have to choose who to run to when the event is over and it's time for kudos. I've had kids tell me that when they went to the parent closest to the stage or the field, the other parent would leave in a huff.

I know these feelings and situations sound complicated, but divorce does complicate your life and your child's life. You'll have some challenges to overcome no matter how hard you work for peace.

If there has been major conflict during your divorce, your

children will have a tendency to take sides. The best thing you can do to discourage this reaction is to refrain from bad-mouthing your ex-spouse in front of your children. Parents need to make divorce final for their children and no longer continue to get angry over the habits and traits they didn't like about each other during the marriage. Although you may need to let off steam, you're only helping to create conflict within your children that will cause problems when they begin to have relationships of their own.

A daughter growing up in a household where the mother complains about the father, for instance, will often marry someone who is frighteningly similar to the man who fits the mother's complaints. The underlying thought process is that the dad has rejected the mother and daughter, so if the daughter can grow up and marry someone similar to the dad and make him love her, then maybe Dad really loved her, too.

TAKE IT SLOW WITH NEW
RELATIONSHIPS

When divorced parents begin to move on with their lives and form new relationships, children may develop new insecurities and anxieties. Not only do these new relationships destroy your child's hopes that the two of you will be reunited, but it also can set him up for disappointments if the new relationships don't work out. Until you both feel that your new boyfriend or girl-friend may become permanent, it's best to keep your adult activities separate from your time with your child. Your child has already experienced a loss, and so in order to save him from going through the process again, don't let him get attached to someone who may be only a brief interlude.

When you feel it's the time to introduce your children to your new significant other, do it gradually, in small increments. Meet for a meal. Don't push it by planning a whole afternoon or evening together. And don't try to give your friend time alone with your child in the beginning. This won't help them get to know each other faster; it will only make your child uncomfortable.

Be prepared for your child to be fearful of this new person taking your affections away. For this reason, don't display affection with your friend when you first introduce him or her to your child. Wait until your child is secure in the knowledge that your having a relationship with someone doesn't change your feelings toward your child.

If you rush trying to form a relationship between your child and your new friend, your child may begin to misbehave or act like a baby to test her ability to get your whole attention. She may be embarrassed by your relationship as well as resentful and anxious. A common complaint would be "I hate it here and I want to go live with Dad/Mom." If this happens, go back a few steps and start again more slowly after your child has had some time to regain security.

Of course, it's best for divorced parents to go on with their lives, but sometimes this can cause their children great anxiety. I had one nine-year-old patient who was brought to my office because he had said he wanted to die. The acute problem he faced was that he had lost his position in the family. Both of his parents were remarried and they both had new babies. He was confused and had developed an extreme case of separation anxiety. His parents were both so focused on their new babies that neither one had noticed his withdrawl until it became serious.

SEEK OUTSIDE SUPPORT FOR YOUR CHILD

If your child is having a particularly difficult time adjusting to your divorce, try looking for support groups in your area. One that has many chapters is called the Banana Split Club. Most often groups like these are offered through your child's school. These groups give your child the opportunity to talk about common complaints and concerns with other children whose parents are divorcing. It's a comfort for your child just to know that what he's feeling is not strange and that other kids are going through the same difficulties.

Your child has lots of new challenges to work through and group counseling can help him. One problem for kids in divorced families is that they no longer have Mom or Dad to act as an intermediary for them. They can't say, "Mom, you ask Dad for me." Suddenly the child is forced to deal one-on-one with both parents.

Even when your child seems adjusted to the divorce, anxieties can arise years later. When it comes time to look at colleges, your child may have old worries return when she has to choose which parent will take her on those trips. Both parents may be paying for college, so whose feelings will be hurt? And even later at weddings, deciding who sits where can be a nightmare. Do your best to ease those anxieties for your child by keeping critical comments about your ex to yourself.

I had a patient who was a senior in high school who became sick at the prospect of having to go visit schools with both of his parents. They still couldn't get along and the anxiety brought on a case of mononucleosis that eventually prevented the trip. Later these anxieties would emerge at parents' day, graduation—any time the boy had to be together with both of his parents.

GET HELP IF YOU CAN'T LET GO OF ANGER

As an expert witness in many divorce proceedings, I have seen more horror stories than I care to relate on these pages. The damage to children is incalculable. At the root of each tragedy is a parent who has forgotten his (or her) responsibility to his child and is caught up in winning a battle. If you imagine all of our emotions as being on a key ring, love and hate are right next to each other. When parents' love for each other turns to hate, their anger can make them forget about the welfare of their children.

If you can't stop seeing red, get some help. You are no good for your child if you're consumed by anger over a failed relationship. When you are healthy, you'll be able to make your child a priority again.

11

Anxiety and Parenting Skills
ALTERING YOUR OWN BEHAVIOR AND EXPECTATIONS

With few exceptions, we learned our parenting styles from the parents who raised us. When two people marry and have a family, they bring together two very different experiences in parenting that have to be meshed into a unified approach to child rearing. This is no simple task. Conflicts are inevitable over punishment for unwanted behaviors and expectations. Because of their own individual backgrounds, parents will naturally react differently to various behaviors or achievements in their children and will envision different consequences and solutions.

HOW TO REDUCE ANXIETY IN YOUR CHILDREN

Setting realistic and unified expectations is the most important step parents can take in order to prevent anxiety problems in their children. Following are some issues I ask parents to address to help them form a unified parenting style.

1. Know Your Child's Temperament.

If you don't know your child's temperament, then you are setting set him up for failure. When both parents understand that

157

they have a shy or anxious child, then they can choose activities accordingly and avoid much pain and suffering. Anxious children may need shorter playtimes with friends. Sitting through the ballet or a baseball game may be more than an anxious child can handle. Make sure you offer choices, and don't force activities that may not be appropriate for your child's temperament.

2. Reevaluate Your Own Well-Meaning Actions.

If you are thinking, "I'm only doing this to help my child," stop and think again. Ask yourself and your spouse the following questions: Am I really trying to help my child, or am I trying to achieve a goal of my own? Consider your child's temperament again. Is what you are asking from her a realistic expectation? Is this something your child can do? Are you being honest about why you're encouraging her to do it? Ask yourself, Am I doing this only to make myself feel better? Is this something I wanted to do when I was a kid? Has my child even expressed an interest in it?

3. Spend More Time on Reward, Praise, and Encouragement and Less on Punishment.

Everyone appreciates reward, praise, and encouragement. It's been said many ways, but you do achieve more through positive than negative reinforcement. Don't make the mistake of playing good cop, bad cop with your child. Both parents need to be seen as being able to hand out rewards and discipline when it's needed.

4. Teach Self-Esteem by Example.

Self-esteem is accepting yourself for both your talents and your faults. If you know yourself, your talents, and faults, you will make good choices in life. The best way you can teach this to your children is by example. If you can't make a mistake without falling apart, then your child won't be able to either. If you can't accept praise or pat yourself on the back when you've done a good job, then your child won't learn this important step.

5. Don't Neglect Your Own Needs.

Adults need to have their own needs met first before they can be good parents. If you aren't happy, then your child won't be either. You can't raise a confident, independent, happy child unless you have built a happy, supportive, accepting atmosphere at home.

EVALUATING PARENTING STYLES

Even when parents sit down together and try to build a unified approach to parenting, it's tough to let go of ingrained attitudes. Following are a number of parenting styles that can contribute to anxiety in children. If you recognize yourself or your spouse in any of the following scenarios and you don't think you can work to change your behaviors, you may need to get some counseling to help you become the parent you want to be.

The Teacher

The parent who gets stuck in his teaching role breeds performance anxiety in his or her child. One such parent came to the dinner table each night with a dictionary in hand. Instead of having dinner conversation, he would call out words from the dictionary and each child was required to give a definition and then use the word in four sentences.

Other "Teachers" are intent on correcting their child's grammar. If they correct too often, they can interrupt their child's thought process, or cause stammering, or eventually make him anxious to speak at all. At first these symptoms may only be exhibited around the parent, but eventually may grow to include all authority figures.

Kids suffering from this type of anxiety problem will soon

learn to abbreviate their answers to one-word general responses such as "nothing" and "fine." These symptoms can be confused with expressive language problems, when in fact the child may be suffering from anxiety because of an overzealous parent.

The appropriate way to correct a child's grammar is after he has finished his thought. Wait until your child has finished his sentence before you offer the correct verb tense.

One of the wishes I most often hear from parents is, "I want my child to be able to talk to me." There is a much greater chance that your child will want to have a conversation with you if each encounter doesn't become a vocabulary or grammar lesson.

I find that many "Teachers" are busy, single parents or divorced parents who don't get to see their children as often as they would like. When these parents do find some time alone with their child, they cram it full of gems of information they think are important. This is a frustrating situation for a child, and he'll often begin to dread time alone with the parent.

The Teaser

Sometimes a parent is a big teaser and a child has a temperament that just can't take teasing. Often the "Teaser" doesn't notice the child's anxiety or notices but thinks the child will get over it if she just gets used to being teased. What happens instead is the child becomes anxious and stops asking friends to come over to the house. She doesn't want to be teased in front her friends, so she avoids this situation altogether.

This situation is usually an issue of a parent not understanding the child's temperament. Most often the "Teaser" rationalizes his (or her) own behavior as trying to get his child to be thick-skinned so she won't get hurt. Again, you just can't make someone get over a fear or anxiety by putting her in touch with that fear. If you don't want a child to get hurt by teasing, you don't tease her even harder. Instead, you stop and teach her alternative ways of protecting herself. After telling your child that you love her and are proud of her, you teach her that she doesn't have to put up with anything that hurts her feelings. She doesn't have to stand around and take it. She can leave the room. When the child's reactions to teasing change, the "Teaser" may realize that his behavior is turning his child away from him, which could bring about needed change from him.

The Anxious Parent

The child of the anxious parent is at a very high risk to become anxious himself. Not only will the child have this tendency genetically, but a parent's anxious behavior will also prompt anxious reactions in a child.

A parent who was shy as a child will often push his own child into experiences that he missed, rather than remembering how painful shyness was and accepting this temperament in his own child. An anxious parent can be very helpful to his anxious child if he will stop to remember what made him feel more secure in various situations and give his child the benefit of his experience. Parents who were anxious as children may spend a lot of time wishing their own parents had behaved differently. Now they have the chance to make those wishes come true with their own children.

At the same time, anxious parents have to be careful not to overprotect a child from situations they find anxious themselves. These parents must keep in mind that the only way their child will learn is through mistakes. They need to let their child try new experiences and challenges at his own pace.

The Perfectionist

The "Perfectionist" parent is all work and no play. She is constantly striving, is highly competitive, is nonemotional, and is impervious to physical and emotional pain. Sometimes a "Perfectionist" has a child who is just like her. Like his parent, this child may be prone to performance anxiety. But when the "Perfectionist" has a child with a different temperament, there are far more emotional casualties. It's very difficult for the

"Perfectionist" to realize that what is good for her is not necessarily good for her child. These children may suffer from a host of anxiety-related problems, from ulcers and irritable bowel syndrome to nail-biting, thumb-sucking, and anxiety attacks.

"Perfectionists" have an especially hard time accepting children with learning disabilities. Many "Perfectionists" were raised in families where great emphasis was placed on having a strong work ethic. Parents who have been raised in such a home tend to interpret learning differences as character weaknesses or laziness.

In one such case the mother of a ten-year-old brought her child to me for an evaluation because her son was constantly getting lost. He had difficulty following directions to the point that he would get turned around in the halls at school, and he constantly forgot where commonly used items were in the kitchen. He was not able to organize, was clumsy, and spilled things constantly. His parents, who had never had learning problems, thought he was lazy and careless.

As it turned out, the boy had a learning difficulty in the area of spatial perception. This can cause all of the problems above as well as making it difficult for a child to read since he has a tendency to skip lines. "Careless" math errors are also a common result of this problem. They don't line up numbers well on paper; their handwriting is illegible. The child had been dealing with this learning disability his entire life, and his perfectionistic parents, who had no trouble in school, couldn't tolerate these symptoms. They came down hard on the kid, which wreaked havoc on self-esteem.

"Perfectionists" need to remember that all children want to do well and want to please until they are about eleven years old. Kids don't become lazy until they are teenagers, unless they have been regularly criticized for something they cannot help. So, when a child seems "lazy" at such a young age, that's a clue that he needs a complete learning evaluation to screen out differences or disabilities.

The Lonely One

A lonely parent, one who isn't over a divorce or has been widowed or is emotionally estranged from a spouse, will tend to overindulge a child and rescue her from all threatening situations because of the parent's own needs as well as his fears that the child will become independent. Such parental behavior can create separation anxiety in children. The "Lonely One" will transmit his own fears of the world to his child, which provokes a general fearful response in the child as well.

In one such case, when the mother finally got over her unhappiness over the divorce and found a new relationship, it was a nearly impossible adjustment for the child. The new man in Mom's life had raised a couple of kids, was not overindulgent, and so his tolerance and understanding of this child's anxieties was very limited. The mother was intrigued by this new parenting approach and was so wrapped up in her affection for this man that she allowed him to put his own expectations on her child.

All of the sudden, a child who had been protected and shielded for four years was forced to deal with a new person who was encouraging his mother to toss him to the wolves.

Look out. This can set up a child for rejection that can result in major depression.

The Abusive Parent

The "Abusive Parent" is usually married to the "Nothing-is-wrong-with-my-marriage Parent," who allows the abusive spouse to criticize and lash out by absorbing the "Nothing-is-wrong" spouse's anger. Growing up in this household, children are fearful of the physical or verbal aggression and watch their passive parent take the abuse without fighting back. This sick relationship produces children who grow up generally anxious and fearful of confrontation. When something goes wrong at school, these children are hesitant to tell a teacher. Instead, they will keep secrets and internalize, and will be helpless to defend themselves in any unjust situation. These children tend to suffer from social anxiety and test anxiety because they're afraid to question or make waves at school or at home. They also suffer from separation anxiety because they don't want to leave the passive parent unprotected.

In this case, the passive parent needs to realize the consequences of *inaction*. Children learn by example and children in abusive households will grow up fearful of relationships. Most often, they'll end up in a relationship that mimics their parents' unhealthy one.

The Drug or Alcohol Abuser

Parents who abuse drugs or alcohol are the height of inconsistency. Sometimes everything bothers them and at other times nothing bothers them, which is extremely confusing to a child. Young kids don't understand that behavior is a result of drug or alcohol use. All they know is that it's impossible to guess what response they're going to get from this parent. This constant state of uncertainty will cause a host of anxiety problems.

The child of a drug or alcohol abuser is typically afraid of drawing any attention to himself. He'll put too much pressure on himself to succeed at school so that he doesn't add another worry to the household. When his anxieties prevent him from being successful, he'll fall apart and may begin to refuse to go to school. These kids will beg teachers not to call their parents; they'll hide notes and forge signatures in an attempt to hide problems at home and problems at school. Kids in these families are also asked to hide family secrets, which only adds to the pressure they already feel.

When the child's problems do come to the attention of the parents, the parent who abuses drugs or alcohol won't see his or her own behavior as part of the problem. I once had a mother bring her child to me for a complete learning evaluation. She was concerned that her child was a "perfectionist" and wasn't making satisfactory progress in school. After thoroughly evaluating the child without finding any learning problems, I began to look beyond her to the family as a whole. Eventually, I learned that the mother was a functioning alcoholic—no one knew except members of the family.

The Unhappy Parent

One of the most difficult cases of school phobia I have ever dealt with involved a little girl who would go to any length to avoid going to school. It was uncovered in working with this child that the parents were focusing on her in order to take the spotlight away from the true problem, which was the difficult marriage. This case required the child's hospitalization to prevent her from hurting herself, a serious approach that shocked the parents into taking a good hard look at themselves. In this particular case, the child got better and the parents got worse and eventually divorced.

This is one of many examples I've seen over the years of how an unhappy marriage can be very damaging to a child. When I hear about parents who are "staying together for the children," I think about this case and how a little girl's life was almost ruined because of such false thinking.

The Immature Parent

"Children are raising children" is a common lament in today's world, but not all of those "grown children" are the teenage mothers you read about in the papers. Many of them are adults who have never grown up and who have not reached a point of maturity to raise a child successfully.

Before we are allowed to drive a car, we have to take a driver's education course, practice, take a written exam, and drive the car for an instructor to demonstrate that we know how to operate it safely. Unfortunately, we don't have a similar system for becoming parents.

The single most important prerequisite to raising a healthy child in a frightening world is to be an adult—a mature, responsible, caring person—who has the ability to give to a child, not financially, but emotionally.

Another important aspect of maturity is being able to recognize your own faults and need for improvement and to take the steps to make those changes for the sake of your family. None of us is perfect. Every parent will have successes and failures along the way. Having the maturity—and the courage—to change yourself and your own behavior can mean the difference between success and failure for your child.

My parting advice for parents is simple. Avoid friendly advice from in-laws, your own parents, friends, and neighbors. Never be afraid to go to a professional—a child psychologist or psychiatrist, child development specialist, pediatrician, or teacher—for help. Examples given here along with prescriptions are abbreviations of true procedures. Please understand that resolving problems takes longer than it does to find the words to describe cases. Be patient and stay actively involved with the treatment program you select. It takes time, sometimes a lot of time to change bad habits and behaviors.

Above all, love your children, support them, and raise them to leave you.

NOTES

CHAPTER 1: OUR ANXIOUS SOCIETY

1. *Journal of American Academy of Child & Adolescent Psychiatry*, September 1990, pages 766–72.

2. S. B. Johnson, "Children's Fears in Classroom Settings," *School Psychology Digest*, 8, (1979): 382–96. H. Orvaschel and M. Weissman. "Epidemiology of Anxiety in Children," and J. S. Werry, "Diagnosis and Assessment," in R. Gittelman (ed.), *Anxiety Disorders of Childhood* (New York: Guilford Press, 1986).

CHAPTER 2: ANXIETY AND TEMPERAMENT

1. A. Thomas and S. Chess, *Temperament and Development* (New York: Brunner/Mazel Inc., 1977). H. H. Goldsmith, "Genetic Influences on Personality from Infancy to Adulthood," *Child Development* (1983) 54: 331–355. D. Daniels, R. Plomin, "Origins of Individual Differences in Infant Shyness," *Developmental Psychology*, 21 (1985): 118–21.

2. Stella Chess, M.D., and Alexander Thomas, M.D., "Temperament and Its Functional Significance," *The Course of Life, Volume II, Early Childhood*, edited by Stanley I. Greenspan, M.D. and George H. Pollock, M.D., Ph.D. Madison, Connecticut: (International University Press, Inc., 1989) pages 163–227.

CHAPTER 3: ANXIETY AND YOUR CHILD'S HEALTH

1. Logan Wright, Arlene B. Schaefer, and Gerald Solomons, *Encyclopedia of Pediatric Psychology*, Baltimore: (University Park Press, 1979) page 421.

2. Ibid., p. 419.

3. F. T. McGehee, Jr., and G. R. Buchanan, "Trichophagia and Trichobezoar: Etiologic Role of Iron Deficiency," *Juvenile Pediatrics* 97 (1980): 946–48. A. P. Orange, J.D.R. Peereboom-Wynia, and D.M.J.

DeRaeymaecker, "Trichotillomania in Childhood," *Journal of American Academy of Dermatology*, 15 (1986); 614–19, 1986.

4. Barbara J. Coffey, M.D., "Anxiety Disorders in Tourette's Syndrome," *Child and Adolescent Psychiatric Clinics of North America, Anxiety Disorders*, October 1993, page 709.

CHAPTER 5: SEPARATION ANXIETY

1. M. Fish and J. Belsky, "Temperament and Attachment Revisited: Origins and Meaning of Separation Intolerance at Age Three," *American Journal of Orthopsychiatry*, 61 (1991): 418–27.

2. Deborah Bell-Dolan, Ph.D., and Tammy J. Brazeal, B.A., *Child and Adolescent Psychiatric Clinics of North America, Anxiety Disorders*, October 1993, "Separation Anxiety Disorder, Overanxious Disorder, and School Refusal," page 564.

CHAPTER 6: TRAUMA-INDUCED ANXIETY

1. Lisa Amaya-Jackson, M.D., M.P.H., and John S. March, M.D., M.P.H., *Child and Adolescent Psychiatric Clinics of North America, Anxiety Disorders*, October 1993, "Post-Traumatic Stress Disorder in Children and Adolescents," page 639.

2. American Psychological Association, *The Child, Youth and Family Services Quarterly*, Division 37, Volume 17, 3 (1994): 6–10, 14–18.

CHAPTER 8: ANXIETY AND THE SPECIAL NEEDS CHILD

1. Interview with Patty Sculley, genetic counselor at the University of Texas Southwestern Medical Center, Maternal Fetal Medicine.

SUGGESTED READING FOR PARENTS AND CHILDREN

Much of the information about stuttering in Chapter 3 came from the Stuttering Foundation of America. One comprehensive guide the foundation publishes is *If Your Child Stutters: A Guide for Parents*, third revised edition, available from the Stuttering Foundation of America, Publication No. 11, P.O. Box 11749, Memphis, TN 38111-0749.

Background information for the discussions of birth order in Chapter 7 came from Dr. Kevin Leman. *The Birth Order Book: Why You Are the Way You Are*. Dell Publishing, 1985.

There are many good birth order books for children to help them understand why the only child feels alone and lonely, the youngest child feels blamed, and the oldest child feels responsible for setting an example:

For the only child, ages five to eight—Marlene Shyer. *Here I Am, an Only Child*. Scribner, 1985.

For the youngest child, preschool and up—Anna Grossnickle Hines. *They Really Like Me!* Greenwillow, 1989.

For the oldest child, ages six to nine—Phyllis Reynolds Naylor. *All Because I'm Older*. Young Yearling, 1989.

Created by Liz Farrington, written by Leslie McGuire, and illustrated by Brian McGovern. *Nightmares in the Mist*. Enchanté Publishing, Copyright 1994. Encourages children ages five to nine to work through their fears with the story of Alicia and Mrs. Murgatroyd's magical paints.

Leo Buscaglia. *The Fall of Freddie the Leaf*. Holt, Rinehart and Winston, 1982. Explains the cycle of birth and death to children ages eight to eleven years old by following Freddie and his friends through the seasons.

Laurene and Marc Brown. *Dinosaurs Divorce: A Guide for Changing Families*. Little, Brown, 1986. Explores the changes caused by divorce in terms that young children, ages four to eight, can understand.

Index

171